In His Hands

True Stories of Wondrous Events in an Unusual Life

Wolfgang Paul Loofs

To my good friend Kathryn on her birthday, from Paul

Victoria, Feb 2023

IN HIS HANDS
Copyright © 2013 by Wolfgang Paul Loofs

First printing: 2013
Second printing: 2016
Third printing: 2022

All rights reserved. Neither this publication nor any part of this publication may be reproduced or transmitted in any form or by any means, electronic or mechanical, including photocopying, recording or any information storage and retrieval system, without permission in writing from the author.

Unless otherwise indicated, all scripture taken from the New Revised Standard Version Bible, copyright 1989, Division of Christian Education of the National Council of the Churches of Christ in the United States of America. Used by permission. All rights reserved.

Photo on front cover: The author and his Beetle on a banana train in southern Costa Rica, Jan. 1958.

ISBN: 978-1-4866-2364-8

Word Alive Press
119 De Baets Street Winnipeg, MB R2J 3R9
www.wordalivepress.ca

WORD ALIVE
—P R E S S—

Cataloguing in Publication information may be obtained through Library and Archives Canada

Preface to third printing:
This third and final edition - ten years after the first - completes the "True Stories of Wondrous Events in an Unusual Life" of over ninety years. Its many ups and downs and equally many solutions to often knotty problems should be a welcome reminder that the Lord guides each one of us according to His amazing plan; trust in Him!

Victoria, BC, Easter 2022
W.P. Loofs

Table of Contents
In His Hands

Introduction	v
Chapter One: After the Crash (1929–1939)	1
Chapter Two: Baptism of Fire (1943)	6
Chapter Three: Foreboding of Things to Come (1944)	10
Chapter Four: Narrow Escapes (1945)	13
Chapter Five: Post-War Chaos (1945–47)	19
Chapter Six: Into the West (1947–50)	25
Chapter Seven: Touring the Old World (1950–51)	29
Chapter Eight: Emigration to Canada (1951–57)	37
Chapter Nine: At the End of the World (1957–58)	49
Chapter Ten: Malgré Tout (1961–62)	59
Chapter Eleven: Once More (1966–67)	79
Chapter Twelve: In Transition (1968–75)	99
Chapter Thirteen: Back to Central America (1976–82)	109
Chapter Fourteen: Studies, Medical Missions, and the Trans-Siberian Express (1983-88)	121
Chapter Fifteen: My So-Called Retirement (1990–99)	131
Chapter Sixteen: Living in Two Cultures (2000–2019)	139
Chapter Seventeen: Sunset (2020 and beyond)	159
Epilogue: Twilight	**165**
Maps	**167**

Introduction

After a friend of mine read my memoirs a few years ago, he commented, "Fascinating, all the things you've done or gone through—but you haven't given God enough credit!" Although I had remarked on several occasions how obvious it was to me that the Lord and His angels had gotten me out of this or that predicament, on reflection my friend was right.

So this little book shall set the record straight by spotlighting a number of events in my life—and you can probably think of some in yours—that without divine intervention would have ended in disaster or other calamitous consequences. These events have occurred over my entire lifespan and give credence to my belief in a personal guardian angel. Other cultures believe that, too; the old Jews knew terrestrial angels, but Jesus revealed that angels act on God's behalf and see Him, and even non-Christians have no trouble accepting this aspect. As Christians, of course, we can derive much support from many Bible verses telling of God's guidance and protection for us, summarized nicely in Hebrews 13:5–6: *"I will never leave you or forsake you… The Lord is my helper; I will not be afraid. What can anyone do to me?"*

Thanks to my exemplary parents, I grew up in a Christian home and thus never had to grope in the dark. I have clung to my confirmation verse—*"Do not fear, only believe"* (Mark 5:36)—and derived much comfort from the above promise in Hebrews. Without that firm footing,

I would likely never have made it through the war and post-war years of my youth, the solo world tours of my middle age, and the charity work and actual living in the third world of my later years, or lasted very long for that matter.

The following chapters should underscore this point and hopefully help uncertain readers put their faith in God, in whose *"book were written all [our] days"* (Psalm 139:16).

—Wolfgang Paul Loofs
November 2012

Chapter One
After the Crash (1929–1939)

It should be noted right at the start that, though I performed military, missionary, and medical duties over many years, I never was a professional soldier, trained pastor, or medical doctor. After the Second World War and its chaotic aftermath in Europe, I immigrated to Canada and had two full-time careers: twenty years in the mining industry and another twenty with the Canadian government. I also had several concurrent part-time jobs: militia reservist, Red Cross and St. John ambulance volunteer, and freelance translator.

I became a student again late in my working life and after retirement, earning several credentials and doing a lot of reading and writing—still, the "jack of all trades, master of none" title fits fairly well. Along the way, I got married in Canada and we had two great daughters; however, barely twenty years later, the marriage ended in divorce. Many years studying alone followed, until I married again, in Honduras, and we have a teenage son.

Up to here, my bio is not that uncommon. What may be unusual is the fact that my divorce, the everyday loss of my wife and children, has opened my eyes to the so-called human condition, meaning that relations among people are more important than our careers, status, and all the honours we crave. Opening your heart to the plights of others rather than bemoaning your own fate is the key to Christian living.

Because of my three unique solo tours by VW Beetle in the late 50s and 60s, I had already seen much of the third world and how so many people have to struggle to eke out a living. Recently divorced and well into middle age, I had to face the likelihood of no more children; therefore, I picked up on an ad for foster children in Central America. That in turn set off a chain reaction of sorts. I became even more interested in Spanish language and culture than I already was, and I visited each of my nine foster children in their respective villages repeatedly, seeing firsthand the real living conditions in those countries, which are among the poorest in the western hemisphere. When my optometrist in Ottawa inadvertently steered me to so-called medical missions, I was hooked. I have been on over one hundred such missions. I found a whole new way of applying myself and what I have learned. It is costly. Volunteers pay their trip and upkeep, but the experience is most satisfying. By interpreting between the poor patients and our doctors, I added to my existing skills, knowledge, and experience in dealing with people of different cultures.

When I now, as an nonagenarian, look back over my rather full life, I can see how many events fall into place, events that at the time seemed to come out of nowhere or were "coincidental." More than ever, I believe that there are no coincidences in our lives: God has a plan for each of us, and sometimes He has to send His holy angels to rescue us from adversity, or even ourselves, so that we can fulfill it.

I also firmly believe what St. Paul famously wrote to the Romans: *"We know that all things work together for good to them that love God"* (Romans 8:28). That includes the fact that I am a cancer patient, as that certainly gives one a new perspective on life, on what is important and what is not. The Bible tells us not only to live a God-pleasing righteous life, but also that ultimately we will be judged on our performance here on earth (Matthew 25:31)—to the extent that we have lived in hope, faith, and charity.

My role model Albert Schweitzer had similar thoughts; however, he was better equipped than I to put them into practice. He was a pastor, musician, and lastly a doctor, blessed with a warm heart and engaging personality—a hard act to follow. But in our respective struggles to help the poor, I share his view that each of us has been given the possibility to alleviate some of the misery despite a rather gloomy outlook for mankind in general.

Before describing the main events of my life, I should provide some background about my parents and early childhood. When I came into this world in Markkleeberg near Leipzig, Germany, in July of 1929—the Year of the Crash, which initiated an economic crisis and ultimately led to WWII—I already encountered my two sisters, Friederun and Hildburg (also known as "Ki"), and two brothers, Walther and Helmut. Ki and Walther had been born in Holland, where Father had represented his German firm for some years and where our ancestors also came from, but I was a genuine Saxon, and the tail-ender at that.

A severe winter followed the hot summer of my birth. As I survived both extremes quite well, I was held to be immune to both heat and cold—a useful quality, if only imagined, for my later life. Of us five, only I am still alive: Friederun lived in Germany, Helmut in Australia, and I, Wolfgang Paul, in Canada and Honduras. This made meeting quite difficult. Walther met his death as a pilot in 1944, and Ki died in 1988; we had been especially close. Meanwhile, Friederun died in 2016 at 95, Helmut in 2018 at almost 92.

My parents were both children of professors but had to go through a lot just the same: Father served the four years of WWI as an artilleryman at several fronts, and Mother as Red Cross nurse, often in field hospitals. They married in 1920 and passed through difficult years of hyperinflation and civil-war-like conditions in the decade that followed. With loans from relatives, Father managed to buy a small house in Markkleeberg in which the family lived for many years—a marvellous time for us children, for we had a big lot with a meadow and trees. In other words, room to run around! Being already five, I needed no playmates apart from my siblings, thus we became close friends and stayed so all our lives, a real blessing.

Mother ran a mini-farm. We had a goat, a dozen hens, and at least one cat. Kids, chicks, and kittens therefore played a big role in our lives as children, as did their adult forms, and we became animal and nature lovers right from the start. All summer, we would run around barefoot at home. The girls wore identical dresses, and we boys identical shirts, all made by Granny to save money.

Those pre-war years were thus pleasant and natural, notwithstanding the ascent of the Nazi Party and Hitler's rise to power in 1933. That first event I remember clearly, because a torch parade went down our main street that January 30, which meant little to me. Economically, the country was going forward and the 1936 Olympics brought prestige. The return of the Saar and Rhineland, and the annexation of Austria and the Sudeten in 1938, gave everyone a lift and strengthened the regime greatly. If only the government had rested on its laurels then!

The only personal event worth mentioning in that period happened when I was seven years old. One of our trees was quite inclined, and my siblings liked to climb on it. When I attempted it, I promptly fell down, suffering a greenstick fracture of my right arm. Therefore I had to ask my grade school teacher for permission to write temporarily with my left hand—which, being a lefty, I wanted to do anyway, but which was forbidden at the time! Incidentally, we still learned to write on a slateboard. We then advanced to pencil and Gothic handwriting, and only later to pen and ink and Roman script. At my time in grade school (1936–39, as I was able to jump a grade), boys and girls entered and left the school building by separate doors; we were a boys class and had male teachers only. Times have changed.

Though my siblings were already in their respective formations of the Hitler Youth (mandatory since 1936 for all youths over ten), I remember my childhood years as happy and carefree. We certainly had much homework and chores to do, but we had enough to eat and time to play. We enjoyed handicrafts, excursions, and family get-togethers. Thanks to good parents and a close family, everything was done willingly and well. We grew up in a Christian middle-class household with a sense of duty, reliability, loyalty, honour, and patriotism. Also parents, teachers, and society in general paid much more attention to good behaviour, order, and cleanliness, and church life played a fairly big role.

My entry into Leipzig's Thomas Gymnasium (which just celebrated its eight-hundred-year-jubilee) was approved for Easter 1939, but then came the occupation of what is now the Czech Republic in violation of the Munich Accord, and on September 1, 1939, war broke out with the German attack on Poland.

My parents in their early sixties, Markkleeberg, Germany 1949

We children lined up at home in Markkleeberg, 1934
L-R: Friederun, Hildburg (Ki), Walther, Helmut, Wolfgang-Paul

Chapter Two
Baptism of Fire (1943)

They say a cat has nine lives. Depending on how one counts, it may be a good thing I'm not a cat! The Second World War (1939–45) was the greatest armed conflict in history, leaving over fifty-five million people dead and countless millions wounded or maimed for life. Casualties from Germany and the former Soviet Union account for half of that horrible total, each losing over ten percent of their populations, as did other European countries. Living through that period, with all its dangers, destruction, and deprivation not only shaped people's lives and outlook but brought home to them God's merciful guidance.

As a young teen in Germany during the war, I was not directly involved in the fighting, save for a day at the end which I will write about later. Yet the war came to all of us. It took a more and more disastrous turn for the country that started the fighting, ultimately turning most of the world against it until the final collapse. The chaos was even worse in the aftermath.

By the end, virtually every family had lost someone at the front—and then the Allied bombing raids on German cities caused incredible devastation, including over half a million civilian casualties. Death and destruction were everywhere. It was hard to keep believing in God's mercy with so many innocent people dying horrible deaths by being burned, asphyxiated, or buried alive—and that with Christians on both sides of the conflict!

We had, of course, heard about the firestorm in Hamburg in mid-1943 and the severe bombings in Berlin and elsewhere, though the official reports downplayed the horrors. The real story could only be heard from refugees from these cities. The authorities stepped up their efforts to prepare the population by holding air defence courses and telling people to reinforce their basements, install fireproof doors, and mark their cellar windows with luminous paint. This last measure was to show rescue crews where to dig in case of emergency. As a Civil Defence messenger, I had to help dig several times in the last few months of the war, which was gruesome.

Meanwhile, I became one of the volunteer fire guards at my school. That meant I slept with a few fellow students in the basement, did my homework there, and could sleep a bit longer since I was already at school. One got paid ten marks per night, thus it was usually not hard to find six volunteers among the fourteen- to fifteen-year-old students. The sixteen-year-olds already did duty at the home AA (anti-aircraft) guns, and at seventeen you were called into the RAD (Reich Labour Service), and afterward—or even directly—into the Wehrmacht (Armed Forces), a process both my elder brothers were already involved in; Father had been called up right at the beginning of the war, serving another six years in addition to the four years he'd served during World War I.

By 1943, the war had been easy-going for us. Apart from some overflights by bomber formations usually headed for the capital, we in Leipzig experienced only minor bombings with a few dozen casualties here and there. Nobody was prepared for what was to come on December 4, 1943 at 4:00 a.m.: the first large-scale air attack on us!

As it happened, on this particular evening only two fireguards had shown up—my classmate Reinhard and I—but the old caretaker Seppl was always there. Initially, our small team had no reason to worry, but then we heard the noise of hundreds of four-engined bombers and our Flak (AA) batteries firing. This time the enemy planes did not, as they had so far, continue towards the capital. Instead, as we found out in horror, we were the target! The British had feigned separate flights to Berlin and Magdeburg and then, once the German defences had withdrawn, recombined and turned towards Leipzig.

The following bombardment lasted, almost unmolested, a good half-hour. It felt like an eternity. The "carpet of bombs" pretty well covered the inner city. Extensive fires and explosions changed the appearance of the city such that afterwards one could barely find one's way! Of course, we didn't notice that until coming out. We sat anxiously in the basement, hoping to survive instead of being buried or burned or asphyxiated. Asphyxiation was a new form of death, which was effected by the air pressure of the heavy aerial mines, and especially by means of oxygen deficiency owing to fires of epidemic proportions.

The principle of a firestorm was fiendish: huge quantities of incendiary bombs, reinforced by virtually inextinguishable phosphorus canisters, started many fires. By dropping scattered heavy high-explosive bombs (so-called block-busters), buildings were destroyed in such a fashion that the various fires could combine into large-scale fire fronts, which in turn sucked the air from the surrounding streets extremely rapidly. The British had already tried this tactic in Lübeck, because its narrow old city core provided an ideal test subject, and then applied it in Hamburg with devastating effect. It was a strategic objective of the Allies to break the population's power of resistance by destroying the residential areas; however, in that they did not succeed, neither in Germany nor in Japan, despite the horrors of Dresden and Tokyo in 1945.

But now it was our turn. At the start, Reinhard and I still looked out, but after the so-called Christmas trees (colourful light markings for the following bombers) appeared and the anti-aircraft fire became heavier, we retired hurriedly into our duty room in the basement. That's where our equipment was: air defence helmets, gas masks, buckets with sands, and flails with water pumps to combat incendiary bombs. These hexagonal rods about one meter long, with a magnesium core which broke on impact, rained down by the thousands, allowing the burning liquid to run out. Several landed somewhere above us, where we could not get to, and a few penetrated all the way to the ground floor, where we could extinguish them with sand.

But then began the horrible roaring of the falling bombs and the deafening din of the following explosions. We sat petrified, listening to the closer and closer whistling of the bombs falling in series, and able to figure out that the next two or three would hit us dead-on. The whole scene is engraved in my memory as one devilish noise: masses of bombs detonate, AA batteries hammer, fragments shriek, powder smell and fire everywhere. I distinctly remember the three (or more) heavy bombs which smashed into the ground in closest proximity: one hit Heine & Co. across the street where my father used to work, another drove into the Lutherkirche (Lutheran church) where I was still a confirmand, and at least one more tore into the "Alumnat" on the other side of the school yard, where the members of the Thomas choir lived. These bombs smashed into the ground at almost the same time, so that the school building was shaken like in an earthquake, and we thought our last hour had come.

Yet here, the guardian angels stepped in. I found myself in a debris-filled hole under the heavy entrance doors which had been yanked out by the air pressure. I was very dirty and totally shaken, but still "utilizable" (as the term was then). Apart from physical pain, the most psychologically shattering and unforgettable experience was the long walk home that morning—it never became "day," the sky remaining murky owing to the large fires and steady rain of ash—through the burning city, the mountains of rubble and streams of refugees forming. Many thousands left the city, miserably "bombed out"—alive, but with nothing apart from the clothes on their backs.

It was afternoon when I arrived in my suburb, finding our house damaged but still habitable, and my mother and sister somewhat distraught but unhurt. We were all relieved and grateful to have escaped alive; after all, there had been two thousand dead and some five thousand wounded that night, as tallied later. In retrospect, I can only thank God, for the likelihood of coming out of this bombardment alive had been minimal.

Chapter Three
Foreboding of Things to Come (1944)

If 1943 had been going badly for Germany, especially in places like Stalingrad, Kursk, and North Africa, then 1944 would turn out to be much worse. In this fifth year, the land war ground inexorably towards its awful end on three fronts—Russia in the east, Italy in the south, and France in the west. The sea war had been lost with the virtual elimination of the submarine threat, thanks to sonar and aircraft carriers. The air war was also won by the Allies thanks to their huge bomber fleets, unlimited fuel, and unhindered production—the very opposite of the Luftwaffe (German Air Force), which by that time could barely take off, though it had jet planes.

Things were equally bad at the so-called home front, as the Allied bombardments, with their "flying fortresses," grew in both frequency and scale—involving as many as one thousand bombers and hundreds of fighter escorts. More and more cities were left in ruins. There was little effective defence: the Luftwaffe had been reduced to a shadow of its former self, mainly due to the war effort in the East and the lack of fuel. The AA guns were too few in number, manned by youngsters and hampered by ammunition shortages. The Civil Defence had no way to cope with the masses of ever-heavier bombs and showers of incendiaries, notably the insidious phosphorus canisters.

One such large-scale attack hit Leipzig on February 20, 1944, when American bombers wreaked havoc in various installations, in particular the famous main railway station, then the biggest in Europe. Over a thousand people died there when delayed-fuse bombs penetrated to the underground areas where many had taken refuge. The Thomas school building, which we had saved by extinguishing the incendiary bombs three months earlier, was now burnt out. While the remaining shell could have been rebuilt, the later Communist regime had it torn down. A new building arose nearby in 2000, on the two hundred fiftieth anniversary of the death of Bach, who had been the choir master there for many years, starting in 1733.

I wasn't directly involved in that school fire; however, another event affected my family deeply. On September 10, 1944, my dear brother Walther died in a training flight when his fighter plane crashed under never fully revealed circumstances. My remaining brother Helmut and I, together with some of Walther's comrades, were the pallbearers. At the funeral, it was very difficult for me, barely fifteen years old, to keep my composure. Yes, I had already seen many dead, killed in the bombings, but this was my own admired brother! To lose him at age twenty and have to bury him was up to then the lowest point in my life, leaving me reticent and pensive for a long time. I still cannot find a satisfactory answer to why it happened. Was it God's will? If it had not been for my devout parents, I might have lost the faith into which I had been confirmed only months before. I was sorely tried already by the military reverses, civilian casualties, wholesale destruction, and general foreboding of things to come.

Just weeks earlier, on July 20, 1944, there had been an assassination attempt on Hitler, which put everybody on edge. Its failure unleashed vicious persecution of anybody even remotely connected with it, and of many that were not (since the Nazi concept of "Sippenhaft"—the liability of one's entire family for the crime of one member—was applied). I can still see the front-page pictures of the hundreds hanged in the aftermath, not to mention the thousands who ended up in concentration camps and/or were executed later, such as Field-Marshal Rommel and Leipzig's former Lord Mayor Goerdeler, slated to head the new government.

Meanwhile, I had been made Civil Defence messenger by police order that year, requiring me to carry reports from one section of the city to another during air raids when the phone lines were out—a high-risk job, indeed! On one such dispatch duty, I walked past an apartment building in Kronprinz Strasse, where my classmate Friedrich lived on the third floor. The building's roof was burning, so I went in to mobilize the people in the basement to fight the fire and/or carry their belongings outside. Friedrich's father was a dentist, and we ran upstairs to save his instruments, at which we barely succeeded. But as I was climbing up a second time, the stairwell collapsed and I fell with all the timberwork to the ground floor. I found myself half-buried in a pile of rubble.

I passed out for a time and couldn't move when I awoke. Soon after, a patrol passed by and looked into the entrance; someone said something like, "Let him lie, he's had it." But I managed to indicate to them that I was still alive. They dug me out and discovered that my right foot was likely broken, or in any case useless. I had to hobble the long way home, where my mother put on a supporting bandage. Still, that limp bothered me for weeks. Yet here again, my guardian angel had kept me from serious harm which almost certainly would have befallen me otherwise, given the circumstances.

Chapter Four
Narrow Escapes (1945)

Life of course went on, though it became more and more difficult as the war entered its final phase in Europe. In view of the continual bombardments of cities at home and the absence of victories at the fronts, a feeling of powerlessness and resignation slowly spread. How could this situation have come to pass, with a self-styled military genius at the helm and armed forces once considered unbeatable? When the air raid sirens wailed, one said goodbye with "Stay alive!" and replied later to "How are you?" laconically with "Thanks, badly, too!" Well, that was the mentality at the time. To the people bombed out, nothing much mattered anymore. What did matter was staying alive, having something to eat, and putting a roof over one's head—we were back to the basics!

After the disastrous defeats in the East and the victorious Allied campaigns in the West, hope for the "final victory" was fading fast, despite the new rockets and a brief success in the Ardennes. One by one, the industrial centres and sources of raw material were destroyed or occupied, and with the last oil from Romania gone and the refineries bombed out, the end was approaching fast. Drastic "total war" measures were imposed, which left no doubt about the critical situation: all non-essential factories closed, military leaves were cancelled, the work week was lengthened, and the remaining manpower pool was "combed through" for the umpteenth time, with authorities on the lookout for anyone who had avoided the war effort thus far. Also, the so-called Volkssturm was created by decree, automatically drafting all men "between sixteen and sixty who are capable of bearing arms." I remember the wording well.

Having qualified in the sea cadets at the required B-level, I was placed in the Navy "Wehrertüchtigungslager" (premilitary training camp) in Mittweida for the four weeks ending at Christmas 1944. People were sent there to prepare for the harshness of war, which included unconditional obedience, physical endurance, firm comradeship, and readiness to sacrifice yourself for the fatherland. We—some six hundred fifteen- and sixteen-year-olds (no females anywhere)—were more harshly drilled than ever before, and we were already used to a lot in the Hitler Youth! We found out quickly that the instructors—mostly decorated or wounded frontline officers—had the task of wearing us out, because that month was very hard, indeed. Morning sports in gym shorts in December and drilling for hours in white fatigues isn't for sissies, especially the continual "get down" and "get up" in half-frozen dirt.

Each morning, we had to appear in the same uniform, washed overnight. The barracks had to be scrubbed spic and span, the bed made per regulation, and uniforms and equipment properly folded and stowed. The daily inspections were agonizing, as the petty officers always found something to complain about. I was once barracks senior and felt everything was in tip-top shape when the inspecting chief flipped the light switch on the way out and exclaimed, "And what is that?"

"Dust, Mr. CPO," I replied.

This resulted in the usual twenty—push-ups, that is.

On the other hand, the nautical and technical instruction was good, given by experts. It proved useful later. We learned, among other things, about tying knots, communicating by Morse code and semaphores, and the flags of all seafaring nations (some forty at the time).

Overall, this tough month strengthened me for pretty well anything life would throw at me later—the intended and worthwhile outcome. I would need to draw on that strength and my confidence in the Lord sooner than I thought.

But in early 1945, one bad news story chased the other: no sooner had the Ardennes offensive been squashed than the Russians launched their overpowering offensive with such masses of troops and materiel that they soon stood at the Oder. We had long had refugees from Silesia billeted with us, but now they came in droves from the Eastern Territories and the Balkans, with horrible experiences of their flight. What one had previously wanted to dismiss as horror stories now became stark reality.

On February 3, 1945, the heaviest air attack on Berlin took place with almost a thousand American bombers, resulting in over twenty thousand fatalities on the ground. It was a terrible prelude to February 13–14, when British and American air fleets destroyed Dresden, already overcrowded with refugees, in three waves in the most horrible way. Between thirty thousand and two hundred thousand people died an agonizing death in what the English writer Alexander Mackie aptly called the "German Hiroshima," leaving all concerned aghast at the manner and extent of its destruction.

That memory, and that of the last cruel weeks of the war, still hurt; one can only supress them. Likewise, to the question "Where was God in all this?" we are told, "We must accept His judgement." Take the tragedy of the *Titanic* and its 1,500 victims in 1912, known the world over—but who knows of the three German steamers carrying wounded and refugees from the East—the *Wilhelm Gustloff*, *Steuben*, and later the *Goya*—which were sunk by Soviet subs, taking ten times as many souls with them into the icy Baltic Sea forty-three years later?

Many terrible things happened then, in particular at the eastern front, where German troops tried desperately to stave off the red tidal wave, while in the West resistance was often only sporadic. Both the soldiers and the populace were more afraid of the Soviets than of the Western Allies, and rightly so. As the two fronts got closer and closer, even boys born in my year—1929!—were called up in mid-March. I went as ordered to WBK III (military district headquarters) in Leipzig, where they issued me my "Wehrpass" (service record book) on March 22, 1945—four months before my sixteenth birthday and barely a month before the Americans marched in. I was classified as fit for service and was to have served three months in the RAD beginning on June 1, 1945, before being assigned to the Navy. It didn't come to that; I can only say, "Thank God!"

But my worries were by no means over. Indeed, I had two narrow escapes. On April 6 and April 10, there were two further large-scale air attacks on Leipzig, and I had to make my rounds above as messenger, regardless of bombs and fire. The dead were temporarily put on the VfB (Verein für Ballspiele) sports field, as the south cemetery was already overflowing. These terrible sights were commonplace and dulled one's sensitivity.

In the last few weeks, there were always fighter bombers in the air, but no alarm was sounded anymore, because it was a permanent state of affairs. They fired on anything that moved, even farmers in the field. They were on "unrestricted hunting missions" and the German side had no defences left. Everybody lived in fear of how all this would end. Schooling practically ceased, but public services continued admirably; they did their duty right to the end.

While the Soviets were fixated on Berlin, the Americans were briskly advancing toward the German heartland—us! I had been ordered by mail to "special HJ duty" on April 6, and a few days later a notice appeared at city hall informing all men between sixteen and sixty that they had been called up "as of midnight tonight," followed by individual telephone calls to Volkssturm personnel. The mailed call-up notices were then ordered destroyed, which may have saved us boys from captivity.

As it became known later, Leipzig was to be defended with three lines, the first one to be manned by Volkssturm units and Hitler Youth from District 107, to which I belonged. Apparently we were to be sacrificed in the open, in front of a theoretical main battle line. However, the bulk of Leipzig's population was war-weary and had no faith in resistance, given the absence of natural obstacles or prepared positions. Rather, they were secretly hoping that the Americans—the lesser evil—would arrive first and thus keep the Russians out. That's how it went, but it didn't stay that way…

In their drive to Berlin, the Soviets basically let the U.S. First Army advance to Erfurt and Leipzig, half-encircling the latter. Of course, we didn't know anything of the tactical events, but one could draw conclusions about the approaching front from the activity in the air, and soon after from artillery fire. On April 16, American advance units were reported only thirty kilometres away, whereupon the order came from District 107 for us to gather immediately at the Schemm school in Markkleeberg. There, we (some twenty boys) were given Flak uniforms and helmets, plus a few rifles and the promise of bazookas, and marched off towards Zwenkau by an incredibly young lieutenant. How my mother must have worried as she, whose husband had already been in the war for nearly six years, whose eldest son had fallen the year before, whose middle son was serving in the East, saw the youngest now leave, too! In retrospect, it was sheer madness, but at the time not everybody thought so: the propaganda kept exhorting everybody to "hold out just a little longer." Surrender, and in particular unconditional surrender, was a taboo subject.

We moved into position—that is, we had to dig ourselves foxholes in front of a heavy AA battery, whose guns had knocked out an American tank just hours before (we could still see the smoke). Unfortunately, this success drew the most unwelcome attention of the U.S. fighter bombers. Those disgusting Thunderbolts, with their wing-mounted machine guns, swooped down repeatedly on the gun positions and fired at us who sat in our holes with pounding hearts, shaken and scared. Late that evening, the promised "Panzerfausts" (bazookas) arrived; everybody got one, and we had been instructed in their use. Then we went looking for something to eat, because we had been given only a little bread. The gunners gave us something, but they didn't have much either.

The night was cool and hardly anybody could find rest. Besides, we also had to stand guard, although we felt protected by the ack-ack gunners. But when the guns were pulled out the next morning, we felt abandoned to a lost cause and disappeared homeward, everybody on his own. We all got away, but I almost didn't make it home alive—my guardian angel had to pull double duty!

I made good progress and was hurrying home already on our street, still in uniform, when an American patrol crossed the little bridge over the Pleisse and rounded onto the street, a good three hundred meters away. One of the soldiers evidently saw me as I was diving through the doorway, because he shot at me. Thank God, the bullet went a little to my right into the wooden porch entrance of our house! There was no time to greet my mother as I dashed downstairs, changed into shorts, and hid the uniform in the ash bin just as the first U.S. soldiers appeared before our house. But a neighbour had seen me returning and now insisted I get rid of the stuff or he would report me—which would have meant captivity or worse. So I had to make the risky trip at night to the river, where several items of equipment had already found their inglorious end. A few copies of Hitler's *Mein Kampf* also floated downriver.

Thus ended the war for me on April 19, 1945. Leipzig finally fell on April 20, Hitler's birthday—but the war would officially last until May 8 in Europe (VE-Day) and until September 2 in Asia. Exactly six years of carnage. What was left of the chivalry, courage, and self-sacrifice with which we had grown up in the following years of racial hatred and aerial bombardments? I myself had "failed" at the last hour and thus remained alive, whereas my brother and millions of others had to die through no fault of their own. Where was the justice, or was this actually God's will? Was it possible to get over all this?

My "Wehrpass" (service record book) issued on March 22, 1945

Chapter Five
Post-War Chaos (1945–47)

While the war had finally come to its gruesome end and the bombings had stopped, thank heavens, the next few years were tough. Yet even in that dark period, the Lord showed mercy on us by allowing my brother to return safely on foot from Bohemia, escaping capture and delivering our father a month later from American captivity, though in very bad shape. Thus for a while we were all together except for Walther.

It didn't last long. Following the Yalta Agreement, pre-war Germany was dismembered: all territories east of the Oder went to Poland (which lost its eastern half to the then-U.S.S.R.), Austria and Czechoslovakia were restored, and the remaining Germany was divided into four occupation zones. The Americans agreed to hand over all of Thuringia and Saxony—our home—to the Soviets and pulled out on June 30, 1945, taking my elder sister, along with other scientists, with them. After an eerie day of quiet, the Russians marched in—and the Iron Curtain descended on us. It would last forty-five years.

Economically, too, these were tough times. We had almost nothing to eat or to buy, state authorities had collapsed, the transportation system was destroyed, and ration tickets were often useless, as there simply was no food available. Bands of released prisoners and freed "East workers" roamed the streets, plundering the depots at will. Basic order was only restored with Soviet soldiers. They behaved like masters of the house from day one, though it was a motley lot that arrived in uniforms and vehicles from all over.

With the old order a shambles, Mother arranged for me an apprenticeship as a bicycle mechanic. My brother and sister worked on now-collectivized farms. Father was unable to work for many months. In the fall, schools gradually opened again, now with leftist (and later communist) teachers, but I couldn't get out of my contract until January 1946—just in time for the intensive re-education campaign in the Soviet Occupation Zone. Apart from incessant KZ (concentration camp) stories in the media, we high school students were taken to a cinema—not for entertainment, but to be locked in and watch KZ films of mountains of emaciated inmates. This certainly drove home the indescribable horror of a political and racial ideology gone mad, of which few people had even known about at the time.

Meanwhile, the "evacuation under humane conditions" of ethnic Germans in the East, stipulated by the Allied Control Council, was in full swing, but utterly inhumanely. In total, some fifteen million people were brutally expelled from their sometimes century-old homes, and two million died in the process. Together with the victims of bombardments and persecution, not to mention the millions of dead and wounded, and many more homeless or displaced, this constituted the greatest human catastrophe in Europe since the Thirty Years War three hundred years earlier.

Germany lay prostrate, totally destroyed, her cities in ruins, transportation and supply systems a shambles, state agencies dissolved. In this chaos, people endured hunger and despair, notably my generation: our world had not only collapsed, but was now exposed as criminal and its leaders soon after put on trial and many executed. What young people like me were thinking and feeling is hard to describe. "Bottomless disappointment" probably comes closest. The fact that most values and attitudes instilled in us were now treated with contempt or even unmasked as lies was hard to digest. Thus we still have today the history-laden term "Vergangenheitsbewältigung"—meaning "coming to terms with the past." I'm sure that Komsomol, the Soviet Youth Organization, members had similar difficulty coping when the Soviet

Union was dissolved—and their system had lasted much longer. Such social upheavals are without a doubt hard on government loyalists.

Then two events hit us hard, and me in particular. One day in the summer of 1946, the younger of my two sisters, Ki, whom I was very close with, failed to come home from her farm work. After a few days, it became clear that she had been "taken away" by the Soviet authorities, a fairly common occurrence at the time. The details of her detention didn't come out until my siblings' meeting in the West forty years later, as inmates had to sign a secrecy pledge. She had found a rusty pistol in the field and given it to her friend rather than turning it in. Somehow that got out, and both were convicted to ten years in a penal camp by a Soviet military court. The camp was Sachsenhausen, the old Nazi KZ under new management, where thousands died, including her friend. Ki survived thanks to her strong constitution and indomitable spirit; she was released in 1950, after more than three years there, when all the Soviet-operated so-called special camps were closed for good. Ki died, still in East Germany, in 1988.

At about the time of my sister's disappearance in mid-1946, my brother Helmut graduated under the special regulations for ex-soldiers and now was itching to get out of the Soviet Zone, since he saw no future there. Children of academics (our father held a doctorate in law) were not allowed to study at university in the Soviet Zone, the new "Workers' and Farmers' State." He managed to get a job offer in the French Zone and thus decided to leave home in July. As I had school holidays then, I went with him to help carry his luggage and sniff Western air. Of course, that was a risky undertaking in those days, with Russian soldiers at the zonal border and much surveillance.

However, the Lord guided us and our prayers were answered, in that we eventually made it into the American Zone, but not easily. We walked, laden with much gear, ever so carefully, some ten kilometres to the first railway station only to be nabbed by a West German policeman on a bike. He finally let us go and we boarded a train to Giessen, where our elder sister now lived. I got there, thanks to my guardian angel, because the American MP checking me let me pass, while another MP took my brother off the train, though we both had the same useless Eastern ID cards. He managed to jump off the truck deporting him to the Russian checkpoint, and we all happily met at my sister's apartment—our last time together for many years. Helmut did make it to the French Zone, but he soon ended up in the Foreign Legion! By the time he was released after six years in Indochina, I had already gone to Canada.

My return trip wasn't exactly trouble-free either. I made plans to visit my godmother Ida's farm, now in the British Zone. I wanted to help her, since her husband was still in captivity, and I also wanted to get some real food. The train ride was uneventful, but at the U.S./U.K. zonal border, everybody had to get out as MPs checked for entry permits, zonal ID cards, and illicit goods—none of which I had. My guardian angel helped me in the darkness to sneak onto the side of people already checked, thus I got through.

By late August, I had to leave for home, and again I had to take the risky way across the border into the Soviet Zone, but this time I got caught. I had walked quite a ways and made it across the border creek. When I stepped out into the road, a Russian soldier on a bicycle stopped me from behind. After a night in an impromptu jail with two other offenders, we were put to work cleaning up the Russians' quarters and yard. Then we were interrogated and searched. Together with a few newcomers, we were marched to the district town and the local commander, who questioned each one of us again, comparing notes. As I was a student and required to be back at school, I was released after two days—but surely with a black mark against my name.

I was soon back with my parents and grandma, whom my sisters had transported seventy kilometres by bicycle trailer from her bombed-out house the year before. I was the only one left of us five children.

The contrast between the East and West grew with the political tensions: the newly formed Bizone (U.S. and U.K.) received Marshal-Plan benefits, while in the Soviet Zone dismantlings continued unabated. Many railway lines became single-track, and entire plants disappeared eastward, including specialists and skilled workers. My uncle Otto died on such a transport to Siberia in 1946 (as we found out much later), whereas my physics teacher came back after years of so-called contract work.

My last year of high school was particularly hard, as we had to complete eleven subjects with three foreign languages: Latin, Greek, and English. We were also the last class of the 750-year-old Thomas Gymnasium. Soon after, it was converted to a regular high school and politically reoriented from Nazi-brown to Communist-red, espousing Marxist-Leninist ideology.

The only good thing in that dreary period of hunger and study—not a happy combination—was the so-called Tanzstunde, a voluntary six-month dance and etiquette course arranged by the parents and teachers of the two senior classes of boys and girls (who in those days were still in separate schools). I knew precious little about girls. Sex was a taboo subject, and "proper" teens rarely met without some kind of scouting. Therefore, getting to know someone of the opposite sex could take a long time. It wasn't easy for me, a rather shy young man, to join, but most everybody else had already, and I do not regret it, though the girl I took a shine to ended up marrying someone else.

Anyway, I passed the gruelling final exams as second-best (which was fine by me; the top student had to give the valedictory speech in Greek) and received my graduation certificate on my eighteenth birthday in July 1947.

But what next?

Working at the American Army depot in Giessen, W-Germany, 1947

The VW Jeep from the Soils Institute, University of Giessen, summer of 1949

Chapter Six
Into the West (1947–50)

I couldn't go to university in the Soviet Zone, certainly not with a father holding a doctorate, a sister sitting in a NKWD camp, and another sister and now my brother already in the West. Besides, the economic and political situation in the Soviet Zone just two years after the war was abysmal: there were mountains of rubble everywhere, destroyed factories and railway stations, continued dismantling, and meagre rations. Above all this was seemingly infinite hopelessness! In addition, Thomas Gymnasium graduates were considered elitist and reactionary, and thus could not expect anything good from the Red authorities; so-called undesirables ended up in the uranium mines in the Erzgebirge (Ore Mountains).

I also felt an obligation vis-à-vis my struggling parents, myself, and indirectly my girlfriend, to make an effort to become independent. Resuming my apprenticeship would not have resulted in any worthwhile income for another two years at least. Therefore I decided, like almost all my classmates and with my parents' approval, to seek my future in the West, especially since my elder sister and brother were already there. Of course, this entailed huge risk. Leaving the Soviet Zone was strictly forbidden, the zonal border was guarded by Russian soldiers, and with Eastern ID cards one could not get ration tickets or a job!

I prayed a lot for advice and confided only in my closest friends. Then God helped me in the form of one of them, my classmate Peter. He knew someone near the border who supposedly could obtain the services of a guide, and then arranged for a meeting in early August 1947. Thus I travelled with that small group—I think we were five, each with a rucksack—by train to Eisenach, to cross the border illegally, near Gerstungen. That was doubly risky, inasmuch as one could never be sure of such guides, whether they would actually take you to the West or back to the Russians for head money. Being caught leaving incurred severe punishment, usually two years in jail. Moreover, the border made a double bend between Gerstungen and Bebra, forcing one to in effect cross twice or make a detour of several kilometres.

Thanks to our prayers, everything went well. We walked all afternoon and evening, led parallel to the railway line on the road to beyond Hönebach, where the guide was paid off and returned. Then we all took the train and reached Bebra without trouble; from there, everybody went his own way. We all had some relatives in the West, separated only by that damned zonal border.

After an uncertain night in the station's waiting room and another crowded train ride, I arrived in Giessen, where my sister put me up in her tiny apartment. First I needed to be legitimized somehow in the Bizone, for a proper refugee processing system hadn't been set up yet, and without Western ID one could not get anywhere. Officially, one could not be registered without deregistration from the previous residence—impossible from the Soviet Zone, a real conundrum!

We listened around for anything to keep me going, and the Lord helped again. It turned out that the U.S. Army sometimes hired German workers for its huge depot in Giessen and they weren't too fussy as to where they came from.

I thus applied to that American base, was interviewed, and then accepted as of September 1947. It was my first job! The administration people of the 502nd Engineer Utility Company, to which I was assigned, gave me written instructions to the mayor's office, following which I received a Western ID card without problem. With that in hand, I could be properly registered as living at Bergkaserne in Giessen, which in turn enabled me to pick up ration cards. What a relief! I could now move freely within the Bizone without having to worry about controls. That alone was worth a lot.

I worked a year and a half with that company, first as a tire repairman, then after obtaining my driver's permit as a truck driver, until the unit was transferred to Bavaria in November 1948 and the remaining civilians were discharged. This time with the Americans would set the stage for later developments, as I can clearly see in retrospect. Not only had I made friends with a GI, but I picked up more English and started thinking about emigrating. For the time being, however, I had to hole up again at my sister's, who had meanwhile moved near Stuttgart.

The overall situation wasn't good. Our parents could hardly make ends meet and were lonely and distraught because of the silence surrounding Ki—the Russians forbade any contact with their camp inmates—and Helmut, from whom only a postcard from Algeria had come many months before, indicating that he had ended up in the Foreign Legion. Visiting my parents (and girlfriend) in the Soviet Zone was risky even with an interzonal pass, because I was of draft age and given the deteriorating political situation between the former Allies. Both the West and the East introduced their respective currency reforms in 1948, splitting the formerly common reichsmark. In 1949, the break was completed by setting up the Federal Republic of Germany (FRG) and the so-called German Democratic Republic (GDR) with their opposite economic, political, and military systems.

I needed to find a job, and fast; again, the Lord helped me in finding work in a steel furniture factory, partly because I could drive their truck and also read blueprints. All the while, I hoped to gain entry to a university, which was by no means easy as few had been rebuilt yet, and six months of reconstruction work was required to be eligible for matriculation, apart from having the necessary funds.

After a few months I quit my job, applied to the University in Giessen, and travelled first to my recently retired godfather Paul, who lived nearby and with whom I could stay awhile. He approved of my plan and offered to loan me a monthly sum to enable me to live and study. So I rented a little room in Giessen and reported to the Soils Institute, as I had met the gentlemen in charge through my sister. God had steered me to the right place: they were looking for a driver and a draftsman. Since I had worked in both capacities at my previous employer, I was taken on as a trainee in May 1949. Moreover, the position qualified as reconstruction work if held to October—the start of the winter semester. Great!

The work was interesting, and my field trips in the Institute's Volkswagen jeep kindled in me such affection for that design that all my four cars later would be Beetles, and in one of them I would travel around the world three times.

Incidentally, VW-Canada has made these trips and the history of that '55 car into a documentary called "Once More" (28 min.), still on YouTube.

That October, I was accepted as a student of natural science. I dutifully studied that semester, and also started the next one, but I wouldn't complete my degree until forty years later—in Canada! At the university, I was introduced to making blood donations at its clinic, then a time-consuming affair requiring a nurse between the donor and the patient operating a toggle switch. Two or three volunteers were needed at a time, depending on the severity of the case. Blood donation entitled one to extra rations, which I could surely use. Incidentally, I have continued as a blood donor in Canada, and occasionally elsewhere, until the age limit and derived much satisfaction doing so; one meets good people at the Red Cross.

Chapter Seven
Touring the Old World (1950–51)

The summer of 1950 found me in the doldrums. My girlfriend had expressed deep doubts about us and my brother had written me from Indochina, which got me thinking whether I should join the Foreign Legion, too.

Just then, something occurred that would greatly influence the course of my life, a "hint from above." A notice appeared on the bulletin board at my faculty at the University of Giessen, announcing the "first student exchange to England to help in the harvest," arranged by the NUS (National Union of Students). As I did not really feel like studying and had neither job nor money, I applied right away and was accepted despite fierce competition. That meant first a long bike ride to the district city for a medical exam and passport—actually a "travel document in lieu of a passport," issued by the military government for Germany—and visas, including for transit and exit!

The effort was worthwhile. I enjoyed the travel abroad and my six weeks in international company near Sandringham in southeast England, though the work was strenuous (picking strawberries is hard on the knees and back) and the accommodation (four-man army tents) spartan. I had grown up anglophile, admiring English fairness and prowess, and would have liked to stay, buoyed by the farm foreman's invitation to come back. But I was required to return to Germany, which I did in a roundabout way, hitchhiking through Ireland and Wales.

Back in Giessen, I had to take leave from the university for the 1950–51 winter semester, partly because I had no money and partly because the Student Committee had held out hope for more exchanges with the U.K. Besides, I was more and more intrigued by the idea of emigrating. I didn't really feel at home in West Germany, and going home to what was then East Germany would have been a one-way trip. Yet England did not allow me in, with the United States it seemed to take forever, and Australia required a sponsor—thus Canada looked inviting. But how to go about it, with no Canadian consulates open yet and no official displaced person or other preferred status? Again, the Lord showed me the way—I just didn't know it then.

Since I had the time, I decided to pay another visit to the parental home in Saxony (I had visited over Christmas without any trouble). I got all the paperwork done, notably a visa in four copies: one each for entering and leaving the GDR, one for the central ministry, and one for me. Soon I was sitting on the interzonal train. The border checks, now done by "Vopos" (people's police) with dogs and mirrors, were thorough, as were the customs inspections; Westerners could only bring small quantities (for example, fifty grams of coffee) and nothing canned. You also had to exchange hard west-mark for soft east-marks at the ridiculous rate of one to one, even though the going rate was one to four, or even five. I had to report in person to the police within forty-eight hours of arrival and departure. That was more risky now since the founding of the East German state: people who had gotten away were considered illegal emigrants.

When I presented myself at the Leipzig police headquarters, again something happened that revealed God's hand. In the anteroom, the police lady told me, "Wait here. Comrade lieutenant will come in a minute." When he came, we recognized each other incredulously; it was Lothar, one of the few classmates who had stayed behind after graduating. I had been able to help him with the final exams, for which he was always grateful. He now reciprocated by telling me privately, "Don't stay the four weeks allowed. Two will have to do!" Apparently my trips to the West, my working for the Americans, and now my journey to England had all been noted with displeasure. I thankfully took his advice and didn't dare until 1967—when passing through as a Canadian—to make a detour to the old home.

I completed my visits and other matters sooner than planned, which was perhaps just as well. My girlfriend wanted a "separation," and I had to say many goodbyes: from her, my parents and sister, several friends, and home itself.

Once back in Giessen, I kept looking for student exchange possibilities. I also kept an eye on the emigration situation. Before long, I had an offer by the Society for Anglo-German Education of London, who had space left for their volunteer agricultural camp at Winchcombe, England, from September to November 1950. Going there would turn out to be amazingly important for my future, for it ultimately led to my emigration to Canada. Much was a repeat of the earlier harvest camp: biking to Frankfurt to get the visas, departure by way of Belgium and the Channel to London.

The camp was populated by some fifty students from Britain, Germany, and later New Zealand. Soon I made two friends: Dorothy, who almost came to Canada but then married in England, and Chris, who would be quite helpful. We men worked hard on the Blakeway & Sons estate, mainly pulling sugar beets and digging potatoes, and I also drove their caterpillar tractor; they wanted me back and gave me glowing references. The trouble was that in those days a foreigner could only get a two-month work permit, and only if no Englishman was available; in practice, that relegated my options to agriculture, forestry, and mining.

The Lord not only had Chris arrange for me to be able to work on the little farm of his aging relatives near the Welsh border, but made me see an ad in the paper looking for workers in Nova Scotia, Canada, to bring in the apple harvest! Thus after finishing the camp and before starting that new job, I travelled to London and the High Commission of Canada, where I applied for immigration right then and there! There was an "assisted passage loan" category, for which one had to deposit twenty-five pounds, with the government advancing the rest. I had managed to save just that much. This application would follow me on my wanderings to Scotland and Sweden and back to Germany, where Canada had meanwhile opened its Immigration Mission in Hanover.

During my time on that little farm (where I looked after the animals, dug ditches, and chopped wood), I wrote to a number of agencies in hopes of extending my residency and work permits. It worked once more. I was accepted for the Concordia Youth Service Camp at Kershopefoot in Scotland, from New Year's to March 1951.

We were comprised of some twenty young men from several European countries, building a forestry road with rock we had to dig from a nearby quarry. It was hard work and we were fairly well paid, but as usual the real payoff was in the comradeship.

Afterward, I had to leave Scotland and the U.K., still without word from the Canadian High Commission in Glasgow. Yet I did receive a telegram stating that a Mr. Tompkins from Canada wanted to interview me in Giessen in early April. Again, help from above! There was little time left, but I managed to return to Germany by a different route, crossing from Newhaven to Dieppe and continuing by way of Paris and Luxembourg, having obtained the necessary visas in London. Unfortunately, it rained often, yet I did see the major sights.

About a week later, this Mr. Tompkins actually came; he was on a tour looking for workers for his enterprise in Fort St. John in the north of British Columbia. When I showed interest, he proposed we travel together to Hanover to the new Canadian Immigration Mission. We did that and caused a bit of a stir there, for Mr. Tompkins spoke for a long time with the consul alone before I was called in. They asked for my file and the twenty-five pounds from Glasgow, after which I could count on "positive news in about three months," now that I had a job offer. The atmosphere with the Canadians was friendly and understanding and appealed to me right away. We parted like old friends. I'm obliged to that man for smoothing the way for me to come to Canada, though I didn't end up in Fort St. John.

While in Hanover, I went once more to see my godparents Paul and Ida, who were relatively close by, to discuss the new situation. Both were in favour of my emigrating to the new land of opportunity. The remaining time was now too short to resume studying or starting a job (even if there had been one), yet it was too long to sit around. On the other hand, I wanted to see more of the Old World before leaving for the new one, for once there I wouldn't be able to come back for years. Thus I hit on the idea to practise geography by cycling through Western Europe.

First I had to ride to Frankfurt to again ask for the respective visas from the Swiss, French, Spanish, and Italian consulates. Once they arrived, I informed the Canadian Mission of my intention to travel for a couple of months, and they didn't seem to mind. I fixed up the bicycle my brother had left behind, a sturdy two-speed model with balloon tires and a coaster brake. I attached two saddle-bags for clothing, two water bottles on the handlebar, and a bedroll on the luggage carrier. I was ready to go! Though I had next to no money (I'd left with twenty-two marks and one pound), I was young, fit, and trusting in God. It was a daring if not foolish undertaking, yet my guardian angel stood by me.

From Giessen I pedalled southward, first to my sister in Swabia, then into Switzerland and France, where I had buddies from the British work camps, near Geneva and Lyons respectively. The other nights I stayed at youth hostels. My provisions were soon used up, and most of my money had been spent on hostel fees. I wanted to reach the Mediterranean and see at least a bit of Spain and Italy; unfortunately, that meant crossing the Alps, Pyrenees, Apennines, and then the Alps a second time. I also had to make up my mind about where to turn back. With God's help, I did complete that circuit of 5,500 km in fifty-eight days, through seven countries (including little Andorra, Monaco, and Liechtenstein), and all that on the above twenty-two marks and one pound! I had been put up more than once by kind people, and also felt the care of the Lord, notably in the following examples.

After visiting the Roman ruins at Nîmes, I reached my first goal: the Mediterranean coast at Sète in southern France. However, I was exhausted from heat and hunger and desperate for a place to sleep. When I asked a farmer near Narbonne for shelter, he referred me to a "travailleur allemand" a few kilometres farther. Sure enough, this German worker was Rudi, a former German POW who had decided to stay in France after the war. He took me in, gave me food, and let me sleep a complete day of rest—and twice, for I stopped there on the way back from northern Spain, too!

Reaching and crossing Andorra was a tough job. On the French side of the Pyrenees, the winding road climbs to over 1,900 meters at the Col de Puymorens, and on the Spanish side to over 2,400 meters at the Ramadan Pass. The gradient became steeper and the temperature colder; I had to do a lot of pushing, no fun in icy rain (and me in leather shorts). Still wet after a miserable night, I sullenly pushed my bike higher and higher, quite alone and hungry. My only consolation was that even with money there was nothing to be had in this remote area. But then I looked down and saw a paper bag, probably tossed out of a car. It still contained half a sandwich—my angel must have dropped it there! I gave thanks and devoured it on the spot.

Though I crossed Andorra practically on foot and in awful weather, my spirits rose as I approached Spain, my dream destination ever since childhood. At the border I had to sweet-talk the guards into letting me enter, as it was true that I had "insufficient means." Still, I made it to Lerida, though I was quite spent. This would be the westernmost point of my journey, and I decided to make for the coast, with Tarragona being the turning point. Once there, I would pedal home by way of northern Italy. That decision made me feel better, but still left me with neither food nor lodging.

Then something extraordinary happened. As I was cycling at dusk toward the coast, several children—sent by God?—ran after me, indicating that I should turn right onto a dirt road. They insisted until I did so and thus I ended up in the tiny village of Espluga de Francoli, where a Spanish-German family lived! Evidently the kids had inferred correctly from my leather shorts and the "D" on my rear fender that I came from Germany, assuming that I wanted to visit that family. These poor people were of course taken by surprise, but recovered quickly. The woman came from Westphalia, and we had a nice evening that turned into a day of rest. The Lord had provided! Thus fortified, I made Tarragona nicely and began the return trip, stopping over again at Rudi's in Narbonne.

I made it all the way across Provence to Monaco and into northern Italy, where I managed to see what I had come for: Pisa and Florence. However, it rained in Venice and I was very tired, having lived on minimal rations and slept only fitfully. Once an Italian farmer gave me some bread. He had been a prisoner of war in Germany and was well-treated; now he wanted to repay his experience. In Milan, I could rest up one day, at the place of another buddy from my English student camp days.

Heading northward through the Swiss Alps, I had to push my bike most of the way up the Bernadine Pass at over two thousand meters, which was arduous indeed and nearly did me in. Again, like in Andorra, my guardian angel dropped a bag with cherries, which helped me reach the hostel at Splügen and thus rest. The last few days were a triumphal ride. I stopped to stay with relatives, notably at my sister's house, before returning to Giessen in mid-July 1951. I was broke and jobless, of course, but with my emigration to Canada pending.

Another hint from above: I saw a notice advertising one spot left for a lumber camp in Sweden, but the deadline was in three days! I applied immediately and was accepted. With a loan from godfather Paul, I was able to travel with a group of German students to Värmland in southern Sweden, cutting and stripping trees with axe and saw for the month of August. After the group left, I managed to stay on alone for another two weeks, as I liked the natural living and general conditions. Only the sea trip across the Kattegat was unpleasantly choppy. On reaching Hanover, I went straight to the Canadian Mission, presented my case, and asked for speedy processing. After all, there was not much I could do now in Giessen except wait for news from the Canadian office.

Working at the Volunteer Agricultural Camp in Winchcombe, England: here unloading sugar beets in Tewkesbury, Gloucestershire, Oct. 1950

Starting the return leg on my West-European bicycle trip, between Tarragona and Barcelona, NE Spain, June 1951

Chapter Eight
Emigration to Canada (1951–57)

It was late September now and still no word, so I applied for yet another Concordia camp in Scotland to start in October. Just then, a letter came from Mr. Tompkins, asking why I had not arrived yet in British Columbia, as the others were already with him! Since nothing was heard from the Canadian Mission and since I couldn't wait forever, I took the night train to Hanover to bring about a decision. On arrival at the Mission, I had to wait until noon due to the crowd while my file was investigated.

Suddenly things began to move quickly. I had another medical exam, security check, and interview with the labour official. He told me that I could travel to Canada with a government loan, provided I committed myself to working for eighteen months in either agriculture, forestry, or mining. He also mentioned that the first two options would be closed until spring, whereas a miner could enter without delay. God gave me a clear choice and opportunity, and I boldly opted for the latter, although I had never been in a mine before. By evening of that same day, October 15, 1951, I was issued a Canadian immigrant visa in my passport! Furthermore, I was assured that my departure from Bremerhaven would take place in early November.

Emigration was suddenly a serious business. After the initial elation, I felt concern and loneliness. In astonishment, I wondered what it would feel like once I was ten thousand kilometres away. For the time being, my parents and sister in East Germany were out of reach, and likewise my brother in French Indochina; thus I could only see my sister in Swabia once more.

A notice then came from the IRO (International Refugee Organization), advising me to be at the IRO camp in Bremen-Lesum on November 2, 1951, ready to ship out! I had to get organized in a hurry: pack my few things in the battered air-raid suitcase, deregister "to Canada," and say goodbye to the old landlady and to Giessen, where I had lived for four years. In the last days of October, I made my final visits to my godparents, and godmother Ida accompanied me to Bremen. I then continued alone to the IRO camp.

The camp was a collection of gloomy barracks fenced in with barbed wire, housing thousands of displaced persons. German refugees and assorted East Europeans, many shabby-looking, all waited for their respective ships. We were divided up six to a room, vaccinated and registered, then left to our own devices—no radio, newspaper, or other diversion. It was rainy and a generally sad time. I was cut off from the outside world, alone with myself. Most everybody wrote farewell letters; I did, too, to all of my family, as well as to my ex-girlfriend. I then waited for the passenger lists and sailing dates.

Finally, there it was: "*MS Anna Salén*, departing Monday, 5 November 1951, for Halifax, Canada." After rather laborious processing, we could embark that day at noon onto that converted freighter of only twelve thousand tons, scarcely bigger than the ferries between Vancouver and Victoria. I was assigned to the lowest deck all the way aft, together with the other five men from my barrack. We soon became buddies. After receiving a meal card and another for toiletries, we were again left alone—there was no lounge or entertainment for the entire voyage.

The actual departure was depressing: a cold and rainy November day, a freighter full with a thousand emigrants, and virtually nobody at the pier. A solitary tugboat pulled the *Anna Salén* out of the harbour, and slowly the coast disappeared, along with Germany, and all of Europe…

By afternoon we were at sea, steaming west on a trip that would take eleven days. My twenty-two years in Old Europe were coming to an end. What would the New World bring? How can I describe the thoughts that went through my mind? Certainly relief that the time had come, but also preoccupation that the venture might fail. God, help me! And He did, as always.

Crossing the North Atlantic on a small freighter in November isn't a good idea, as any old salt can tell you, but we had no choice. Though I had recently sailed the Channel and Kattegat (and would traverse all oceans except the Arctic Ocean in the next fifteen years), this first long sea voyage sticks in my mind as the most exciting and adventurous one. On the first night, already the choppy Channel caused many seasick people, with obvious consequences for the cleanliness on board. The next day, they offered fifty cents a day for volunteers to help clean up the mess; I was one of the few takers and would thus step ashore in Halifax with five bucks! At a stop in Le Havre, we took on another five hundred passengers, the total now being 1,500, making for a crowded ship. At noon, we lost sight of the Normandy coast, bitterly fought over only seven years ago. Bye-bye, Europe.

The next week is quickly told. We experienced increasingly foul weather, culminating in a seastate 10 to 11 storm for two days and nights. The little ship rolled and pitched, everything not tied up slid around… hardly anybody dared to go on deck, not even the sick ones, thus it was quite a mess below decks. Sunday, November 11 passed without service or memorial. It was cold and clammy. After one week at sea, everyone was fed up, tired, and seasick or nearly so. How had previous generations of emigrants endured their much longer voyages?

While approaching Labrador, we had sleet and hail, and the cabins were not heated. There was nothing to see or do except think about what lay ahead. The weather moderated a bit as we passed south of Newfoundland, but the tension rose after ten mostly rough days.

Then, finally, the New World was in sight! We felt like explorers discovering a new coast when we dropped anchor in Halifax, but we couldn't go ashore yet. In the afternoon, the first workplaces were assigned, but we roughly three hundred miners had to wait our turn, and nobody knew beforehand where he would end up. In a slave-market-like atmosphere, the immigration officials called out, "We need six men for Sydney, Nova Scotia" or "Four men for Val d'Or, Quebec" and so many for here or there. But I had dreams of mountains, lakes, forests, and Indians and we twelve cabinmates all wanted to go West. So, when Winnipeg came up, we all volunteered to go to Flin Flon from there, which nobody had heard of before. That was the last night on the now quiet *Anna Salén*.

Friday, November 16, 1951 was the big day of my official arrival in Canada as a landed immigrant. With passport and train ticket in hand, we went down the gangplank to the large customs hall of Pier 21 (now a national museum), where hundreds of hesitant newcomers lined up, wondering what would come next. Our little group was processed quickly; we then walked around a bit in the harbour area before boarding the waiting CNR train in the so-called colonist class for the trip to Montreal. The next day, we changed onto another CNR train bound for Winnipeg; we were fewer now, as many had left in Quebec. Travelling across Ontario, we heard that we may well be going beyond Winnipeg, and on arrival there the incredible happened: we were shown a telegram from the Ministry of Labour ordering us to proceed to Nelson, British Columbia—exactly where I had wanted to go!

So we switched to a CP train, marvelled at the Prairies and the Rockies, and got off at Nelson, where two Cominco pickup trucks were expecting us six (the other six had left in Edmonton). We had to split up, three going to the Bluebell Mine and the other three—Frank, Sven, and me—to the HB Mine near Salmo. There we were put into eight-man tents and began working the next day, November 22, 1951.

We started aboveground, digging foundations for the future staff and bunk houses, but I also had to "help" in the kitchen, which meant many extra unpaid hours before and after regular shifts. After Christmas, I was promoted to underground labourer and, upon hearing that there was a shack available in nearby Sheep Creek, the three of us rented it. This was more economical than paying half one's wages for room and board. Initially we lived very frugally, sitting on powder boxes and sleeping on cardboard, until the folding beds and tools ordered by mail arrived and we could fix things up. We had power but no water, which we fetched from the creek. We used an outhouse and walked several kilometres to and from work—a dicey prospect at night because of the cougars.

Yet things were looking up. Much to the surprise of the Cominco accountant, I was able to make my last loan repayment after only six months (as opposed to the eighteen months allowed). Also, I took the St. John First Aid course at the mine and passed it very well, which was noted. Then I was detailed, as I had requested, to go on the next course for prospective miners in the spring, when we had to learn and practise all kinds of mining activities for four weeks under the watchful eye of a mining inspector. Having earned the British Columbia Blasting Certificate, I could undertake contract work. That meant pairing up with another miner—for safety reasons, one works in pairs underground—to drive a drift (tunnel) using a limited amount of materials for a specified number of meters in shifts, a risky but potentially profitable task.

Mining was and is dangerous work. In the eight months that I toiled underground, two miners suffered fatal accidents, and several more injured themselves or had to take time off due to gas poisoning—this in spite of the fact that we already had some protective clothing, helmets, and headlamps. In those days, one still took a candle along to warn of carbon monoxide gas if it went out. Cominco was safety-conscious—after all, accidents are costly—and staged competitions among its various divisions with prizes for the one with the least accidents. When I twisted my foot while unloading a tipper car so badly that I could hardly walk for days, I was assigned to cutting safety fuses in the powder magazine. That way, the incident wouldn't show as a lost-time work accident.

On another occasion, I would have been a goner if my guardian angel hadn't been sent in the nick of time, in the form of my partner, Russell, who reacted quickly and to whom I will always be grateful. He was an older Irishman, usually quiet (but who could on occasion swear loud and long), with whom I enjoyed working. He was a competent miner and glad to have found in me a blaster, enabling him to share in better-paying contract work. On that particular day, we had removed the broken rock from the previous shift, drilled and loaded the new boreholes, and ignited the safety fuses, of which the shortest would take four minutes. That was calculated to provide enough time to reach the ladder leading down to the next level and thus to safety before all hell broke loose above: thirty-five explosions releasing tons of rock.

Although I had performed this sequence many times before, this time I slipped from the oil-coated ladder, almost falling into the chute where the blasted rocks thundered down a few minutes later! To make matters worse, my lamp had been torn off. Russell was two paces behind me and leapt to grab my outstretched hand, pulling me out. We reached the floor at the same moment as the explosions went off above us! This brought back memories of the air raids and my Civil Defence messenger trips, and I thanked God for once again sparing me.

Thanks to my better earnings and to simplify the long hike to and from work, I bought my first motor vehicle: a 125-cc BSA motorcycle with all of four horsepower. I had passed the driving test on my neighbour's little Austin and thus had the licence before the bike was delivered. For the next three years, I used it not only to go to work, but also on weekends and holidays to explore the interior of British Columbia, on sometimes incredible dirt roads, as far as Jasper National Park. Meanwhile, I had been offered our tiny house in Sheep Creek at an affordable price, and I acted quickly: I was a house and property owner overnight! Even if it was by European yardsticks only a simple hut in a remote area, it was the beginning of fifty years of home ownership in Canada.

More importantly, I also saw a ray of hope in respect to a future career: my likeable underground boss Roy let me know that Cominco would soon be looking for candidates in its assayer-training program. It would start in the fall and I was qualified, as high school graduation was a prerequisite. I applied in the summer and was then summoned to the head office in Trail for a lengthy interview. Evidently I had made the short list of nearly a hundred applicants. In mid-August I received the exciting news that I'd been accepted, starting September 15, 1952, for a two-year contract! That meant I had to entrust my little house in Sheep Creek to the tenants and look for a room in Trail, no easy matter while still working forty kilometres away at the mine where Russell and I tried manfully to finish the contract. We didn't quite make it, but earned well. At the Assay Office, I made less money but was now a salaried employee and thus rid of union problems.

We four successful applicants—Len, Jim, Stu, and I—were assigned to the four major work areas—wet lab, zinc plant, fire floor, and lead/zinc analysis, on a six-month rotation each. In addition, two evenings per week we studied Applied Chemistry. Both activities were checked and graded every six months, and the outcome determined the next wage increase. Thanks to the new work and attending night classes together, we soon became good friends. We even went on outings together in Len's small car. I also took a course on geology and prospecting, and thus had four full evenings. My laboratory experience from Giessen was useful, but I still had to learn the complicated English and American system of weights and measures, not to mention lots of formulae. I have long forgotten the details, and today most of that work is done by automated equipment. But overall I was suited for the tasks and had reason to believe that I'd found a career with good prospects after only one year with Cominco. I remained with that company for twenty years before becoming a public servant. I celebrated the completion of my year in the mine with my first blood donation in Canada.

Once I discovered the Lutheran church in Trail, I attended there. I also saw an ad somewhere for so-called pen pals, and soon I had several, for I had always been interested in foreign countries and cultures, especially in the Latin world. With one, Carmen in Madrid, I wrote for many years; she not only was a good language teacher, but also became my soul mate. We shared the same birthday. Sadly, she died suddenly of a brain stroke in 1970. I am still in contact with her sister.

In 1953, I took the big step of buying my first real house! The shack in Sheep Creek hardly counted as one, and I had a tough time selling it, as the mine was to be closed. What I got was a little bungalow with two rooms, a kitchen, and a bathroom in Rivervale, a hamlet ten kilometres from Trail on the Columbia River. I had to take out a bank loan, but I paid one-third in cash. That got me the house, but nothing in it, so I had to buy the most needed items, including tools; with those I could make furniture myself. When I was about to buy a small fridge, the dealer suggested rather to my astonishment that I should pay for it in instalments, although I had saved money for it. He explained that this would establish my credit worthiness! This was good advice, since North America lives on credit, today much more so than in those days—which I'm sure it will come to regret, both in private and public life.

The 1950s were a golden period for Canada, and for me as well. The economy was growing rapidly, as Canada had become industrialized as a consequence of World War II and the Korean conflict. Construction was everywhere as soldiers returned to their civilian jobs, and the population increased by means of a baby boom and immigration alike, up 50% in the 1951–71 census period to twenty-one million.

Life then was almost idyllic. Mr. and Mrs. Average Citizen (married, of course) wanted nothing more than a little home, a couple of children, and if possible a car. The birth control pill and street drugs didn't exist yet, foodstuffs were by nature organic, materials reasonably priced, tools and appliances uncomplicated, and electronic devices not invented yet. Canada enjoyed international prestige, and the public service and the military—even the general population, except Quebec—were still quite British in character. This would change drastically in the following two decades, as American influences, Franco-Canadian self-confidence, and Asian immigration all increased considerably.

I was doing all right myself, now well into my training contract with Cominco in Trail. Long-term employment was practically assured; after all, the company operated a large smelter, with some four thousand employees. The work in the lab became more complicated and we handled a lot of dangerous chemicals. Acid burns occurred often, and one trainee passed out while working with H_2S gas. Only the house in Rivervale proved a disappointment; it had been built cheaply, without a real foundation and proper septic tank. It took a lot of money and effort to fix both shortcomings.

Around that time, a colleague persuaded me to join the local army reserve unit, in which he already served. It was possible for immigrants after two years in the country and with a declaration of intent to become a citizen. I was happy to provide that and thus joined—or so I thought—the artillery unit, which together with the engineers was housed in the new armoury in East Trail. I had completed the geology course, and the two army training evenings fit between my chemistry classes, thus it was manageable. I felt military service for my chosen country was the honourable thing to do. The paperwork for foreigners went ponderously through Pacific Headquarters in Vancouver, however. All the while I continued my duties, which included training on the new radar-controlled anti-aircraft gun.

Six months later, I was ordered to the Battery Commander, who told me that my application to enlist had been refused, because I wasn't yet a Canadian citizen, and I was thereby dismissed. The message from headquarters stated specifically that I was under no circumstances to be allowed on the new AA-gun or the radar course—which I had just successfully completed. Awkward! Since I could not be officially enlisted, I could not be formally discharged either. All the months I had served thus did not count and never were paid.

However, in September 1955, when militia training started, I did report to the engineer unit. Thus I could join the engineers, as they "had nothing confidential." But promotions there took longer on account of the trades courses required, and officers needed an appropriate degree. Ironically, in the early 1960s the artillery unit in Trail was disbanded, and in 1972 I was commissioned as an officer with the engineers in Ottawa, when I had acquired sufficient qualifications. I was discharged in 1982 as a captain and remained in the Supplementary Reserve until 1994 (my sixty-fifth birthday). Altogether I served almost forty years, I never had to fire a shot in anger. Thank God!

By this time I had passed all phases of the assayer training program at Cominco, including the two semesters of chemistry, and the provincial examination in Victoria was scheduled for early in December 1954. Even before then, Len and later Jim were sent to company mines in Tulsequah and Kimberley, and Stu decided to return to Ontario, leaving me as the only candidate. Thus I had to make all the preparations and take the lab equipment to Victoria by myself. The practical exam was held over five days in the government laboratory, and three evenings covered the theoretical aspects. I managed most everything quite well. After a supplementary in May 1955, I received the Licence as Assayer in the province of British Columbia. Now I had to help the new candidates along and was given the job of doing the lead and zinc control analyses, an exacting task with much at stake. When I had done this work satisfactorily for five years, I was transferred to the Technical Research Centre, a respected position which I held for another twelve years.

But back to my guardian angel, who had been waiting in the wings. Having paid back my study loan as well as the mortgage on my house, my next project was to buy a car. In terms of price and technology, the Volkswagen Beetle was the only contender. I sold my beloved motorcycle as a down-payment and ordered the car in May 1955, rewarding myself for the assayer licence. I could pick up my Beetle in Vancouver and drive home through northern Washington, thanks to my newly acquired U.S. visa. Unfortunately, this first car was ill-fated from the start. On a weekend trip back to the HB Mine, it slid down a soggy embankment, ending up on its side and bending the door frame. The accident seemed to occur in rather slow motion—the angels slowed the slide! However, I didn't have insurance yet and still owed half the purchase price. Moreover, I had to walk to work for two weeks while the repairs were made. Yet worse was to come.

I had been invited to visit the family of Lloyd, a mining buddy in southern Saskatchewan. At first, the long trip went as planned as I drove through the magnificent Waterton-Glacier National Park. I wanted to reach Regina that evening and I almost made it—but for a pickup truck which turned onto the highway from a drive-in theatre, sideswiping my Beetle in such a way that it overturned, ending up on its side on the pavement. Here the Lord protected me again. There were no seatbelts in those days—the guardian angel pushed me between the seats, thus protecting me. I was only shaken up and had briefly blacked out when the collision occurred. But the car was now irreparably twisted and thus a write-off before it was even paid for! Since a police cruiser was among the cars that had been driving behind me, there was no shortage of witnesses. The driver of the truck got fined and lost her licence for a while, whereas I received a new Beetle from the insurance—again a grey 1955 model. With that car I would circumnavigate the world three times, and it would be exhibited at the Canadian National Exhibition in Toronto and in Montreal in 1968. (see "Once More" documentary by VW-Canada on You Tube.)

In His Hands

Over the next few years, I became well-established. I had a steady job at Cominco, a little house in Rivervale, and a car in the self-built garage. I was a reservist in the militia, and now—after the then-mandatory five years—I became a Canadian citizen! But no wife or family yet.

Working underground at Cominco's HB Mine, Salmo, BC Apr 1952

My house in Rivervale nr Trail, BC and new Beetle, Fall 1955

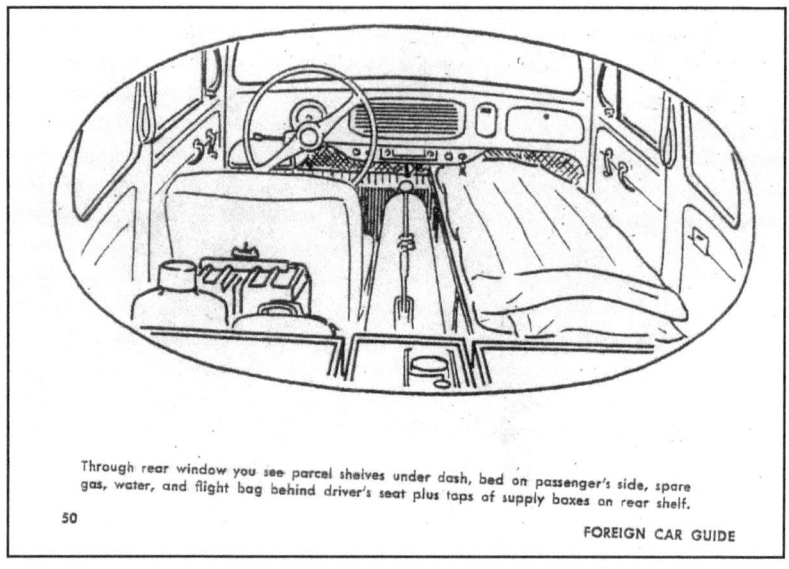

Interior of my 1955 Beetle converted into a camper for long-distance travel (drawn by the author and published in "Foreign Car Guide" of March 1965)

Chapter Nine
At the End of the World (1957–58)

In that happy time of cheap gas, little traffic, and no dependents, I went on many camping trips on my holidays and long weekends. The western part of North America, from British Columbia and Alberta to the U.S. Southwest, became my hunting grounds; my Beetle sported the name "Lone Ranger" on the side. I experimented with different configurations for sleeping and cooking in the car, so as to be independent of campsites—a precondition for a trip to South America. This idea was now taking shape in my mind with a car rather than a motorcycle. I had gotten wet too often. That exploratory trips to foreign lands have educational value is undisputed, but now I had an additional impetus: my brother would be in Peru in the spring as part of a French film team (they were to record footage of the native peoples in the region); meeting him there was the big attraction. I had saved a month of holidays, and asked for and was granted five more months of unpaid leave, giving me December to May.

A so-called Pan-American Highway already existed, but several sections—notably in Central America and Northwest South America—were incomplete (one, the "Darién Gap" between Panama and Columbia, still is not finished). As there was no other route through Brazil then, and as I did not fancy going back and forth the same way, the idea of returning by way of Europe was born. All that depended, of course, on obtaining the necessary information and documents, and getting the preparations done in time. These latter included converting my Beetle into a camper: fitting a homemade plywood cot lengthwise on the right side by removing the passenger seat and rear bench. The space gained now accommodated two jerry cans for gas, a plastic jug for water, and a couple of boxes for engine oil, tools, and emergency rations, as well as a gas stove. I had also bought a complete spare wheel besides the two extra tires. It's amazing what all fit under the hood! This arrangement proved so effective that I kept it practically unchanged for my following trips, too.

Of course, everything had to be done as cheaply as possible, for I had no earthly help whatsoever. On the contrary, I took pride in doing everything by myself, armed only with much faith in God, trusting in the Lord with all my heart (Proverbs 3:5). Evidently, nobody from Canada had driven alone through Central and South America and returned in the same car; it would be difficult even today.

I left Trail, British Columbia on December 2, 1957, and drove in a southerly arc across the Rockies and midwestern plains to the Mexican border at Laredo, Texas without trouble. While initially the cold was bothersome (the heaters in early Beetles were notoriously poor), beautiful mountain scenery and later southern mild weather compensated for it. Even driving through Mexico wasn't too demanding, except for the heat and annoyances due to a different culture. For example, I had taken a hitchhiker along for a whole day who wanted to see his sister and had promised a good meal there. When he finally got off, asking me to wait, he never came back—and my watch was gone, too. On the other hand, a kind Mexican paid to fix my flat tire when he heard where I came from. Thus one's impressions balance out: good and bad coexist everywhere.

I departed Chiapas with my car and me on a train, as the road connection on the Guatemalan side of the border was still under construction. Indeed, Central America—with its many borders, currencies, mountains, and gaps in the road system—would be quite challenging. New Year's Day found me entering El Salvador, already ten thousand kilometres from Trail, but my admiration of lakes and volcanoes was somewhat spoiled by another tire blowing out. The country is only three hundred kilometres long (it would seem much longer on my bicycle tour twenty-five years later), so I could traverse it and also pass through southern Honduras quickly on my way to Nicaragua. Once there, one had to report in person in the capital—much like back in East Germany. But when I arrived at the office, it was closed for the Epiphany holiday.

I drove down to the coast for a dip, then decided to pass the night at that secluded beach, which was a beautiful place. I prepared a little supper and went to bed contentedly in my car, lulled to sleep by the murmur of the ocean. How good it was to know that my guardian angel never sleeps; he certainly was on duty that morning, waking me up at dawn to splashing sounds. My Beetle stood up to the rims in floodwater! Evidently I had parked at low tide, and now had to get out fast. Fortunately, I had packed two short plywood planks with me for negotiating muddy sections; thanks to them, I was able to retreat little by little onto firmer ground. This incident was scary, and it could have ended my trip if I had remained stuck…

My next concern was reaching Panama and South America proper, as there was no land connection. My next destination therefore was Punta Arenas in Costa Rica, from where an American ship went directly to Panama, or I could take a local boat to Golfito, which was much cheaper but later required rail connections. Eventually my car, and another one containing a couple with a lapdog, was loaded onto the tiny *Don Fabio*—a scary undertaking at dusk! Next morning, both vehicles were transferred onto flat-cars of the Ferrocarril del Sur, for a romantic ride through hot banana plantation country. We endured another transfer to the narrow-gauge flat-cars of the Chiriqui Land Company to the actual border.

Once there, the authorities would not allow the other car in because of the dog—and as my Beetle was lashed down on the same flat-car, I was caught up in their predicament! After a day of haggling, I was allowed to leave, onto another train to Concepción, Panama—all told, it took three different railways and five days to make just a hundred kilometres; one has to grin and bear it and rely on the Lord for help. At least I was on the highway again, and with little to see except the occasional glimpse of the Pacific, I was soon in what was then the U.S. Canal Zone.

I was stuck there for almost three weeks, but that was a welcome break, for in the Zone the roads were maintained, utilities worked, and it was clean and safe. While trying to find passage to Colombia, I had my car checked and made friends with three American sergeants of the JWTC (Jungle Warfare Training Centre) who helped me in several ways, even letting me stay with their families when my ship was delayed. Perhaps they were angels in uniform?

After a night at the pier, my Beetle and three other cars were hoisted on board the *MS Colombia* and in the afternoon we put out to sea. We passed through the Panama Canal and after two nights on deck and one day of sailing, we docked in Buenaventura, on Colombia's Pacific coast. I had arrived in South America!

Unfortunately, the political left and right in Colombia had become such enemies at the time that civil-war-like conditions were the norm. Especially dangerous was the region southwest of Bogotá, where I needed to go to get the visas for the next few countries. The drive from Cali through the West Cordillera was difficult, and from there to Ibagué was doubly risky, with sharp curves and steep slopes on the one hand, and the possibility of attacks on the other—one could see cars with bullet holes here and there. However, with God's help, I made it both ways; I was stopped several times by army patrols who searched the car but let me go each time, with a warning not to dawdle in the area. That compelled me to keep at the wheel until late, when I could finally risk camping off the road.

All the driving now took place in the Cordilleras between two and three thousand meters in altitude, and over narrow unpaved roads devoid of passenger cars. Everywhere I went, my presence caused a stir. When I asked a soldier at a crossroads for directions, he got in with me, and I delivered him to his home in Pasto, to the joy of his poor family.

A high point of travelling through Ecuador was, of course, standing at the actual Equator—which I did for the first time just north of Quito after a tough drive through the mountains at carnival time, when the locals celebrate with sometimes rowdy music and much alcohol.

Over terrible roads I reached Cuenca, but now a problem arose: the road section to Peru had not been built yet—one had to travel by boat! After a rapid descent, the road to the sea changed into a muddy field, in which a tipped-over bus was already stuck. I managed to get through to Puerto Bolivar only with great difficulty. Here the Lord sent me an angel in the form of a nice Peruvian named Jorge, who wanted a ride for himself and his suitcase. After looking around and negotiating all day, we finally found a skipper willing to take my car and both of us to the Peruvian side near Tumbes. Driving onto that open barge on transverse planks at dusk was scary enough, but driving off the planks at night and up a steep muddy bank was even worse. My quiet prayers were answered!

Yet the five kilometres to the actual border were the worst. The mud was so deep that, despite all evasive manoeuvres, I ended up getting mired; that meant walking back to hire a truck. Although that truck also got stuck, with the help of several men it was freed again and then towed me in the direction of Peru. But as a result of our efforts, we looked like veritable pigs! After customs clearance, we could clean up in the local "hotel" and resume driving south the next day on a real road—until we came to a wide river without a bridge! With hasty prayers and floating in the car—with a Beetle, it can be done—we got across, the angels having pushed! At Piura, my passenger got off, and I continued through hot bushland and desert to the capital, Lima.

I had financial and technical concerns: the waiting periods and sea passages had been expensive, and the bad roads and towing were hard on the Beetle. Yet there would be help in Lima, and I also expected news from my brother at the Canadian embassy. Helmut had arrived with his small team and was filming not in Peru, but in Tierra del Fuego. He expected me to meet him there before the end of March! This required a slight change in plans, since I now had to proceed all the way to the tip of South America. With the car fixed and me rested, I set out to traverse two long countries. I still had seven thousand kilometres to go. It was easy leaving Peru, but awkward entering Chile due to much red tape and a second customs check far inland. It was closed when I reached it.

I was now twenty thousand kilometres from home, with half my money and time gone—and I had to get back home somehow, too.

One can appreciate how long Chile is—a good four thousand kilometres—after driving for days over endless gravel roads through the Atacama Desert, the world's driest region, towards the capital. The

Pan-Am Highway had not been paved yet, and the washboard grooves ran so deep that one either crept along slowly to protect the vehicle or flew above them at high speed, inviting damage to the suspension. The shimmering heat and the clouds of dust complicated matters, especially when a large nitrate truck approached—recalling the Crusaders' wail of "many stones and little bread."

The real problem was the toll those roads extracted. Soon I had a flat, and exchanging tires in the heat was no fun. Worse, there was no place to repair it. I was now in Antofagasta Province, carrying on through the stony nitrate desert, marked by the almost complete absence of human habitation, just the odd passing ore truck. No sooner had I gotten some radio reception and was enjoying some old country music than the recently repaired spare tire blew. Another tire went flat the next day—three flats in as many days! This was serious, for I no longer had any spare wheel left, and was also low on gas, with both jerry cans used up. The Lord helped me make it to Copiapó, where I could fill up and have one tire repaired. The other one was a write-off.

In the capital, Santiago, I was told that there were no flights available to Punta Arenas, but that one should be able to make it by car in a week. I couldn't be certain that Helmut would still be there, but at least I could write him and also obtain the visa for Tierra del Fuego. The die had now been cast, and trusting in God's guidance I began this final leg on good roads and in pleasant climate.

Soon I would have to cross the Andes into Argentina, and I decided on the lowest of the three passes, Paso Tromen. Consequently I turned east beyond Temuco to Villarica and its namesake lake, beyond which the road deteriorated considerably, turning into a stony path at the border. Though the foothill landscape was beautiful, the entry into Argentina was difficult. First came a narrow, bumpy forestry road, then an adventurous crossing of the lake by means of a wooden ferry loaded with horses, and finally a winding path to Junin de los Andes. But the quick formalities, friendly people, and glorious scenery were fine compensation. The twisting dirt roads and mountainous countryside soon gave way to a highway through first a hilly region, then flatland: the famous pampa lowlands, with sagebrush, cool breezes, and much solitude.

In spite of a broken shock absorber and frosty weather, I had reached Santa Cruz and was able to cross back into Chile via the border—a little shack in no man's land—before nightfall, parking along the Strait of Magellan for the night.

The next day, March 25, 1958, will always be fresh in my memory. It was mild and sunny, with a good view of the strait and surrounding glaciers. A strong wind was gusting and kicking up much dust on the gravel road; therefore I had to drive slowly, if only because of the many sheep everywhere.

Then it happened: a cloud of dust appeared from the opposite direction, approaching and shrouding a jeep inside it—here, halfway between Punta Delgado and Punta Arenas, at 53°S, the end of the world? Both vehicles stopped, then reversed toward each other, and lo and behold it was my brother Helmut with a Monsieur Delaborde of that little film group! I cannot describe the joy I felt at our first reunion after twelve years. The inscription on my Beetle's hood, "Fe en Dios" (faith in God), had borne fruit. The goal and high point had been reached, but also the turning point. After a week we had to separate.

As there was no ship leaving soon, I had to commence the long drive north to Buenos Aires. Ten days later, I arrived there and eventually managed to get space on a French ship sailing within a week for Lisbon, Portugal. I would thus return by way of Western Europe. However, how to get back to Canada before my prearranged holidays ran out was still an open question.

The Lord works in wondrous ways! First I had to go to the Canadian embassy to obtain a new passport, as all pages of mine were full of stamps. I was received in a very friendly way, handed my accumulated mail, and the passport matter was handled efficiently. The next few days were filled with visits to consulates and travel agencies, among them Canadian Pacific Airlines. The people there were most helpful and cabled the Liverpool CP office, which soon replied that their *Empress of England*, sailing on May 30, would take both me and my car. All this fascinated the CP agent to the extent that he notified their PR man, a Mr. Tatton. He was sceptical at first, but after verifying my travel account he asked me to return the next morning for an "interview." That turned into a splashy affair, with half a dozen reporters from as many newspapers firing questions at me in English, Spanish, and German. Even a TV man was there filming us! That evening, I could see myself on TV in Mr. Tatton's home, and the next day I read articles about my travels in all the major papers of Buenos Aires. I also had my Beetle readied for the European leg, with Volkswagen picking up the cost.

On the day the ship was to depart, I drove with Mr. Tatton on board to the official end of the Pan-American Highway in the city centre of Buenos Aires. I had stood at the official beginning of it in Laredo at the Texas border with Mexico four months earlier!

My car was then loaded, and soon I was off on the voyage to Lisbon, and thus Europe.

The seventeen-day voyage was enjoyable, with calls at Montevideo, Santos, Rio de Janeiro, and Las Palmas before dropping anchor in Lisbon on schedule. After unloading and customs clearance, I was off again in my trusty Beetle, first to Sevilla and a three-day side trip through Morocco and Gibraltar, and then to Madrid for a brief visit to my pen pal Carmen and her family.

In mid-May, I was in Germany again, and there the Lord would give and take away. He gave me a joyous and somewhat daring rendezvous with both my parents and my sister Ki in what was then West Berlin, into which I had flown. They had managed to come for a day. The Lord had taken away the girlfriend of my youth, who went on to marry someone else.

The return voyage from Liverpool to Montreal by sea, and then across Canada in my Beetle, went without mishap (despite tiredness), and I arrived home after six months and over forty thousand kilometres overland. It was one of the most significant periods of my adult life, and though two similar world tours would follow, this was not only the longest but in some respects the most memorable. It gave me increased faith in God, because without His help I would have been in a real fix several times.

Moreover, I came to appreciate His creation—our world—much more, as only extensive land and sea travel can bring about (space travel had not been invented yet). In addition, I felt deep gratitude for the many acts of assistance which ordinary people, often VW personnel but no doubt guardian angels, had offered me, thus reviving my belief in the essential goodness of people.

For the first time at the Equator just north of Quito, Ecuador Jan 1958

My Beetle on the barge in Puerto Bolivar, S Ecuador, Jan 1958

Entering Chile and the Atacama Desert, Mar 1958

The brothers meeting on the road nr Punta Arenas at the southern-most tip of Chile on March 25, 1958

Chapter Ten
Malgré Tout (1961–62)

There had been some changes on the home front since my return from that first world tour. Apart from getting back into the work routine and my reserve duties, and fixing up the property, I had to sort out personal matters. Lots of correspondence was due, not only with family but also with people who had helped me, and with new friends. Among them were two nice young women, one Colombian, the other Flemish, whom I had met along the way; however, I managed to lose touch with both of them.

To clear my mind, I used my summer holidays of 1959 to make a demanding trip all the way up to Fairbanks—I like and need to be alone in nature from time to time—and thus I could legitimately say that I had driven to both Alaska and Tierra del Fuego, likely the only Canadian at that time to have managed it. Yet a year later I met, in the company cafeteria of all places, an attractive woman from Germany. After some legal hurdles and much paperwork, we married three years later and had two lovely daughters.

Cominco had recently promoted me to lab technician, a morale boost but also unhealthy, as I was employed in arsenic purification. Thank God, I suffered no lasting ill effects. Then came good news from my brother: he had in short order completed his doctorate, proposed to his girlfriend Sigi, and received an offer from ANU, the Australian National University. The fact that he and Sigi (married now) moved to Canberra in 1961 gave rise to the idea of visiting them. I had been thinking of travelling to and across Africa anyway, so why not add on an Australian tour?

That was the era of the progressive decolonization of Africa. More and more visas were required, yet they were hard to get. Some of my visas had very low numbers: Upper Volta was 52, and the Central African Republic was 15.[1] One needed not expect heavy traffic in those parts!

It should be mentioned that preparing a world tour in the 1960s required an incredible amount of correspondence with consulates, offices, and shipping agencies, and this time I would cross three oceans. Just then, in the fall of 1961, the unfortunate wall separating East and West Germany was thrown up, as some three million East Germans (I among them) had already fled to the West. It would stand for almost thirty years.

I got the six months off work (five unpaid) as requested, albeit with difficulty, from late December 1961 to early June 1962. The result of having my car checked out was unpleasant; the drive wheel was worn and compression mediocre. Repairs would be laborious and expensive, out of the question now. Therefore I would have to chance it, relying on the Lord's guidance.

I had no illusions about the difficulties of this undertaking, especially in view of the state of my Beetle and my finances, not to mention the political situation in Africa and the personal risk. The plan was for me and my car to go by freighter from New Orleans to West Africa, drive across to East or South Africa, catch a boat to Western Australia, drive to Canberra to meet my brother, and then return by boat to Vancouver. It sounded simple, but not on a budget of two thousand dollars! The mode of travel was thus predetermined. As on the South America trip, it involved sleeping and cooking in the car and being as independent as possible by taking along a large water jug, two jerry cans for gas, an extra wheel, and two spare tires.

With my wife and child safely ensconced at its godparents in Vancouver, I set out alone on December 21, 1961, on what would

---

[1] A country's visa numbers reflect the number of other travellers who have been issued that same visa in a given year from the same consulate.

become a series of tough tests for both steed and rider, but with faith in God (the car now sported the logo "malgré tout," meaning "in spite of it all"). The journey seemed ill-fated from the start, though in the end it proved a great success.

My departure was delayed a bit as the self-timer on my camera quit, forcing me to get a new one, otherwise I couldn't take "evidence photos" along the way. Driving across the Rockies and through the Midwestern states was difficult, what with snow and ice and cold, but the trusty Beetle ploughed through—except on Christmas Eve in Iowa, when a passing truck pushed me into a snow bank and I couldn't get out by myself. I had to walk back quite a ways to call the Automobile Association; they sent my guardian angel in the form of a Mr. Anderson, who not only pulled me out but took me to his home to share supper with his family, a nice treat!

I reached New Orleans on schedule, only to have to wait two more days to have the Beetle loaded onto the Delta Line's *Del Monte*, a 1944 Victory freighter in mediocre shape. It was to be my home for the next three weeks. I was the only passenger, and initially nobody paid any attention to me in that allegedly first-class cabin. Well, who in his right mind would want to go to Africa in those uncertain times? On December 30, 1961, we weighed anchor, but not heading for my destination, Conakry in Guinea, for which I had booked, but for Freetown in Sierra Leone, for which I had no visa and which would add a few hundred kilometres to my travels. The reason was political. The new state of Guinea had let the Soviet Union use Conakry as a naval base. Therefore, in those Cold War times, U.S. ships could not enter its harbour.

The entire week was frittered away still in American waters, loading cargo in Houston, Port Arthur, and Lake Charles, where another day was lost due to rain, when rice could not be loaded. On January 6, 1962, we finally headed to sea, past Key West and considerable destroyer activity: the Cuban Missile Crisis was about to break out! After a few days, our bucket was practically alone at sea—and I with my thoughts.

The voyage itself was uneventful. There was nothing for me to see or do except read or sunbathe. Owing to our slow speed, we arrived a couple of days late, and it was uncertain if or how my car and I would be unloaded, leaving me worried when the *Del Monte* dropped anchor in Freetown on January 23.

Nobody seemed to know that or even worry about my situation. At long last, a representative of Delta Lines came on board and told me among other things that one could drive to Conakry by car. That afternoon, my poor Beetle was unloaded with ropes onto a barge, which took it and me to the pier, where I slept in the car. It wasn't until the following afternoon, once the formalities were dealt with and I had some money and gas, that they let me drive off—then I promptly lost my way. There was no map, and no signs!

The first night in Africa was like it is often described in books. I was in a jungle clearing, amidst all sorts of noises, and in great heat. In the morning, I had to deal with a flat; it seemed I had parked on a branch with long thorns! This would be a taste of things to come in the next ten weeks travelling through eighteen African countries. Lots of technical difficulties and many surprises (usually nasty) were ahead. However, the Lord would extricate me from these troubles time and time again.

First, I had to get to Conakry—the beginning of the euphemistically named "Trans-Africa Highway." I was amicably processed out of Sierra Leone, but treated as somehow suspect on the Guinean side. The customs officials went through everything. Then some kind of chief passed in a black Mercedes, and I noted how much respect he commanded with the people.

Someone explained to me that nobody was allowed to camp or obtain gasoline without this district governor's authorization. Sure enough, I was soon escorted to his house for an interview and then taken through dark alleys to the "guest house" where I was to spend the night. It was scary at first, but my guardian angel watched over me. With a twenty-litre gas allotment, I made it to Conakry; however, beyond Kindia the road deteriorated more and more and it got so hot that I quit driving at noon for fear of overheating the engine. When I reached the Niger, the ferry had already shut down for the day. I took a swim (dangerous, I was told afterwards, for the river was wide, fast, murky, and full of leeches) and then camped amongst monkeys and vultures. The next day was very hot again, and I had to make several detours around impassable sections and bridges, but eventually I made it to Mali.

Here the border officials were nicer, and the obligatory audience with the district governor, a Monsieur Cisse, went well enough. But when I wanted to drive off, the engine wouldn't start. This was an embarrassing situation—stuck in the West African desert! In this unlikely place, the Lord sent me three angels. First, Monsieur Cisse promised to find me a truck to tow me to the nearest VW garage—in this case, in the capital Bamako, a good 150 kilometres away. And he delivered. I stood in front of that garage at midnight, and the driver was happy to be paid with the American cigarettes given me on the ship. Then there was Monsieur Georgel, the manager of the SCOA (a French transportation company) agency dealing with VW, Berliot, and Austin. He was a clever man, determining that my drive wheel had indeed worn out and needed replacing. Amazingly, he just "happened" to have a cannibalized Beetle engine sitting there—the Lord provides! He put his mechanics to work taking mine apart and installing that drive wheel from the other one.

Just then, a Unimog drove up from which a German alighted. It was Dr. Beinhauer, who had also studied in Giessen and ran a veterinary station nearby. He took me to the station and let me rest until my car was ready to roll the next afternoon. Though I got off lightly, this repair bill and the unexpectedly expensive gas made a big dent in my finances, and I was only in the third of eighteen countries! Upon my return to Canada, I sent letters of thanks to all three of these human angels, strengthened in my belief that there are no coincidences.

As I made my way across West Africa, there were other surprises, good and bad. The going was tough, as reflected in my diary entry for February 3, 1962:

> Mood at zero, road bloody awful, speed 15 km/h, losing oil, shocks worn, and only one-fifth of the way; no car can endure that for long—Lord help me!

And He did, again and again. After crossing the now-wide Niger, I entered Niamey, where I got gas, a letter from my brother, and an opportunity to wash in a little spring nearby. Yet neither the car nor I were feeling all that well; the former had to be pushed several times until I got it fixed in Kano. Later, at Maiduguri, the gas station attendant told me that the road to Fort Lamy (now N'Djamena) in Chad was open again. That was important news, for it meant I would not have to travel through Sudan, with its four-wheel-drive requirement, but could instead cut diagonally across a bit of Chad, the western Central African Republic, and the northeast Congo to Uganda. But this route would lead through some of the hottest and most desolate areas of Africa, not to mention the political unrest and poor road conditions. Still, I would have to get through there somehow, and with the Lord's help I succeeded against all odds.

I had to pass through a bit of Cameroon and nobody took any notice of me, except for some natives who were mesmerized by my leather shorts. Entering Chad was unpleasant because of the difficult approach to the ferry across the Chari and the high fee. However, family mail at Fort Lamy boosted my morale, which I would need in the tough weeks ahead.

The trouble started with a terrible dirt road, with deep sand and many potholes caused by trucks. There were no passenger cars here! When a native woman with a water jug on her head waved me over and I stopped to take her to her hut, four more came, and I ended up carrying all five for nearly ten kilometres.

There were vaccination controls, because the water had become contaminated due to inundation by Lake Chad. This meant boiling the water, and that in more than 45°C heat. I also had to contend with improbably deep grooves in the dirt road, complicated by broken drainage pipes. Moreover, there were no signs, gas stations, or traffic for that matter along this long stretch.

Then the inevitable happened: with a loud noise, I sank into a deep hole, right behind one I had been able to avoid. I hadn't seen it because of the tall elephant grass. I got my car out of that ditch only with some difficulty, then took stock of the damage: oil had sprayed out, luggage was tossed about, a rim was dented, and the shocks and muffler were damaged. But incredibly, the trusty Beetle was still running. Thank

God! I cautiously carried on to Fort Archambault (today's Sarh) and recovered in the customs shed, disused thanks to the customs union with the Central African Republic.

The next day, faced with a two-hundred-kilometre stretch to the CAR border, I somehow managed to lose the "highway" and thus continued adventurously over third-class side roads through deepest inner Africa, and alone. I saw what no tourist will ever see: tiny villages with round huts and well-built natives (prey for early slave-hunters) with spears and naked children.

Then I had another breakdown. The fan belt was broken! Since with great foresight I had carried a new one with me, I was soon underway again, otherwise I might have been stuck for a long time.

Thanks to my jerry cans, two days later I made it back to the main road near Fort Sibut. At some point, I had entered the Central African Republic without being aware of it. The next stretch was better, and so I reached the junction at Bambari in good cheer. I gave a lift to another hitchhiker for the Elim Evangelical Mission, dropping him off by evening. A Swiss missionary couple let me sleep there as well—the first of several Christian mission stations that would shelter me, bless them! Thus strengthened, I continued through the jungle to the Kotto River to wash and so entered the border town of Bangassou, only to discover that the customs house was already closed and that there was no gas to be had until the next day. Also, my concern about the situation in the Congo, which I would now have to cross into, hardly let me rest.

The former Belgian Congo had at that time three governments: the official central one in Leopoldville (now Kinshasa), whose President Lumumba had been murdered shortly before; the Tschombe administration in separatist Katanga; and Gizenga's rebel regime in the East Province and the District of Paulis—exactly where I needed to pass through! In view of Lumumba's murder, the general unrest in the country, and massacres of whites in various parts of Upper Congo, utmost caution was required. A man alone in a small car would be just the thing for the marauding bands, the missionaries warned me. The only way to tackle this predicament was to completely trust in God, for there was no going around, and certainly no going back! And the Beetle must not let me down, though it was also tired; it had a cracked valve shaft, unreliable distributor, and leaky muffler.

The endeavour started right away with problems. The ferry across the border river Bomu didn't get going for want of a twelve-volt battery, whereas my Beetle only had one of six volts. I returned to Bangassou, where I had spotted a Mission of St. Gabriel. Its Canadian director, Pater Myron, organized help, and eventually the ferry chugged across, depositing me on the Congolese side. The customs people first were suspicious of me, then became friendly and referred me to the police station at Monga, sixty kilometres onward. The official there regretted that only his chief could register me, and as he was just out, I would have to wait. I did that at the mission in Monga, where the pastor couple Holte took me in. I want to mention here how selflessly I was put up for the night at six mission stations in Central Africa. I have since thanked each one in writing; sadly, several of these missions were later destroyed and most of the missionaries killed!

The sûreté (police) chief returned the next day and issued me the necessary "laissez-passer" certificate. Thus I could still catch the ferry across the Bili and reach Bondo. Similarly, I got over the big Uele by ferry and continued to Buta; at both places I passed the night at the respective mission stations. But I had to present myself at both an army post and the sûreté, where after a long wait I obtained the permit and bad but expensive gas, as well as some provisions. After another night with missionaries (this time Anglo-American) near Titule, I found myself on the road east, towards Uganda!

After driving through coffee plantations and cotton fields, I did arrive in Poko all right, but I couldn't find my way to Paulis. It turned out that the main bridge had collapsed, necessitating an awful detour. Some people asked me to take a patient with me to Paulis, and I agreed on the condition that they help me get gas—suddenly twenty litres became available. The youngish male "patient" seemed quite healthy, and didn't really know the way either. It became an eerie drive at night in fog, and we often had to ask scared inhabitants for directions, but my guardian angel guided me to Paulis. Again I hassled with police; I got their stamp, but no gas. Finally I did obtain some, and could thus carry on happily through hilly terrain and pygmy country to just before Mambasa, where police stopped me but eventually let me pass.

I would have liked to turn off into what was then known as Albert Park, but had to drop this idea; it was just too risky. Besides, I was tired. At dusk, therefore, I drove into a clearing to camp, but a group of some thirty wildly gesticulating pygmies, armed with bows and arrows, surprised me and put me to flight, my guardian angel having helped me to get in the car and start it in a flash. I had to keep driving to the relative security of the police station at Mambasa, where I could finally get some rest.

My patience was sorely tested at the military governor's office there. I was referred from one officer to another and, though celebrated as the "first tourist since independence," I was subjected to a very thorough examination. Everything had to be taken out of the car and put on the street. I went along with this, joking with the policemen, and was allowed to return my possessions back into the Beetle, minus of course a few small items.

Following that ordeal, I was on my way towards Beni, higher and higher into the Ruwenzori Mountains (the area of Jane Goodall's well-known gorilla research). Surprisingly, good quality gasoline was available in Beni, so I filled up and started on the bumpy road towards the border, confident at least in that respect.

Despite warnings of elephants, not to mention rebels, I covered a fair distance. I set up camp amidst sheet lightning and slept fitfully at the edge of Albert Park, no doubt watched over by my guardian angel.

The next morning, the last day of February 1962, I drove to the border station at Kasindi, where I had to wait a long time, together with several trucks. That made me contemplate the odds of getting out scot-free; but lo and behold, I was eventually checked out without much fuss, and thus left the dangerous Congo in one piece. Naturally, I felt quite relieved and most grateful to God, His angels above, and the missionaries below.

Still, my difficulties were far from over.

In Uganda, still British at the time but about to become independent, I could finally observe African wildlife in Queen Elizabeth Park. I saw hippopotami, elephants, water buffalo, and all kinds of exotic birds in the wild, alone in God's creation—something that is impossible today, except on safari. Moreover, for the first time in many weeks, I could camp without undue worry.

Incidentally, I crossed the equator several times in those days, as it runs across the border and through the park. There was a sign on the main road to Kampala where one could literally plant one leg in the northern hemisphere and the other in the southern hemisphere.

By now it was high time to head south and find a ship to Australia. So I hurried to the next big town, Mbarara, from where I could sent a telegram to my wife, telling her of my safe passage through the Congo and congratulating our daughter on her first birthday. After passing two interesting days with an Indian family and a night at the Catholic Mission Mitala (with a German, Canadian, and Belgian pater), I continued on to the capital, Kampala. I was concerned about my car and getting space on a boat, as everybody wanted to leave British East Africa, with independence coming for all three components—Uganda, Kenya, and Tanganyika. The Lord was with me, though. After some failures, I was able to book passage to Australia on a Dutch freighter leaving Durban, South Africa in three weeks.

But the findings in the VW garage were unpleasant. Among other things, the Beetle's frame head was cracked and the brakes worn. However, I could afford only the most pressing repairs and had no time to waste. I still had to cross almost nine thousand kilometres to reach Durban!

Thanks to good roads, I got to Nairobi quickly. There, I picked up my mail and discovered that many of my cards and letters from West and Central Africa hadn't arrived—not surprising, given the chaotic conditions. Equipped with a retread tire, I set out again, now southward to Amboseli Park and into Tanganyika. I could see Mount Kilimanjaro, except its peak, which was shrouded in clouds.

There was no time to detour to Serengeti Park, so Tsavo would have to do. I turned onto the gravel road leading to the park's entrance and was almost there when my trusty Beetle, with an audible crack, sank at the right rear. Unfortunately, it wasn't just another flat tire, but a broken torsion bar! That was truly serious, a consequence of the horrible roads, and I had no choice but to limp back to Nairobi, a good two hundred kilometres in the wrong direction, taking it nice and slow, for if the other side were to break, too, the journey would end! Here again, the Lord (and later, Volkswagen) came to my aid; I managed the laborious return trip in twelve hours, and the mechanics at Coopers Motors VW could scarcely believe it. It takes a lot to break a torsion bar! They installed a new one and charged me only for the parts.

The dirt road to the Tanganyikan capital Dodoma (the city hall still bore the German imperial eagle and the year 1912), notably the ascent to Pienaar's Heights, was quite a challenge due to mud and rough patches. Following the advice of some Rhodesians I met, I took the short route south via Itigi to Rungwa; however, I had to ford the Berea river, the Beetle making gentle waves, led by my guardian angel.

After surmounting the high pass to Mbeya, I crossed into Northern Rhodesia (Zambia), glad to have the dubious roads of East Africa behind me. On the other hand, the eight hundred kilometres of gravel of the Great North Road along the Muchinga Mountains still lay ahead; after that, all main roads would be paved.

Indeed, driving went well now, but then it began to rain heavily and all through the night, turning the remaining route into a mud field. As stopping was out of the question, I was dead tired by the time I reached the junction at Kapiri M'poshi, and thus the paved main road. Close to that junction lay the town of Ndola, where only months before the U.N. Secretary General Hammarskjöld had died in a mysterious plane crash.

While having my car checked out in the capital Lusaka, I wired the shipping line and was told that my boat would not be in Durban until April 3 and would then sail to Cape Town; therefore, I decided to go all the way to the Cape. After visiting Victoria Falls and Rhodes' grave near Bulawayo, I entered the Republic of South Africa at Beitbridge. In Johannesburg, I learned that my freighter, the *Straat Singapore*, would sail on April 9 from Cape Town directly to Fremantle, in Western Australia, so I booked right then and there.

Now I had time for a leisurely trip to Durban and the scenic drive through the Transkei, along the coast of the Indian Ocean. Eventually I found a nice location for camping and swimming at Morgan Bay, where I was alone and stayed for two days—the second of which nearly became my last. I had gone for a walk along the rocky shore and ventured into the water when two successive waves threw me so hard against the rocks that I thought my legs were broken, or worse! Thank God, they still functioned, and I crawled to safety, dazed but alive. My guardian angel had done its job! To add insult to injury, on the way to Port Elizabeth I had another blowout, this time a total loss; both the tire and tube were beyond repair. That left me with only two spares, but they would have to do, as my funds were shrinking alarmingly.

After a detour to Cape Agulhas, Africa's southernmost point, and passing through the wine region of Paarl, I entered Cape Town as planned on Sunday, April 8. My boat was expected the next day. I took in the sights, camped at the cape, and on Monday proceeded confidently to the harbour. However, my ship was a day late and my car couldn't be loaded until the day after that. This necessitated an extension of my entry permit as well as a new passport, as mine was again full of stamps. When all was done at the Canadian embassy, I returned to the Cape Park for what I thought to be my last night in Africa.

However, it seemed that Africa did not want to let go of me yet. When I wanted to leave in the morning, the engine wouldn't start by any means—and only hours before my allotted loading time. I was sixty kilometres from the harbour! I had to walk back to the emergency phone and call the Automobile Association. My angel made someone come quickly; he established that the starter motor had broken down, then pushed my car to start and escorted me to the VW garage. By afternoon all was fixed, but at an unpleasant cost.

At the shipping office I was told to come back the next morning, which meant spending another night in my car. But this time I parked closer to the harbour, where I had already spotted the *Straat Singapore*. I was allowed on board the next afternoon (fish had to be loaded first), and the Beetle followed a day later, much to my relief. We now had a place to stay for the next two weeks, and Australia and my brother awaited me!

I left Africa with deep gratitude to the Almighty, His angels, and the people who had helped me out of several predicaments. Thanks to them (and the tenacity of car and driver), I had achieved what seemed impossible then and almost certainly hasn't been done by anybody since—crossing Africa alone, from west to east to south in a much-tested Beetle in just eighty days (à la Jules Verne). The African journey had covered 18,500 kilometres, and how challenging they had been!

The following sea voyage was pleasant and proper. The nine other passengers were all British ex-colonial officers from East Africa, and the Dutch captain made us welcome. Leaving Cape Town around the Cape of Good Hope is always dicey, however; when passing through the infamous mixing currents of the South Atlantic and Indian Oceans, our little freighter rolled and pitched so much that everything not strapped down tumbled around or slid back and forth. The inclinometer showed twenty-three degrees that night, but the international guardian angels were on duty and kept us from real harm. Apart from the albatrosses accompanying us, we saw no living thing, or anything else for that matter, during the entire voyage. The only and welcome interruption was our sighting of the French Amsterdam and St. Paul Islands, which the captain had intentionally steered close to, halfway through the two-week trip.

We arrived in Fremantle on Friday, April 27, 1962, and at first things went smoothly. The Beetle was unloaded, the Automobile Association was notified, and mail was obtained. But then a big muddle came up. The AA carnet allegedly sent from Cape Town had not arrived yet. Also, any car arriving from Africa had to be fumigated, and insurance was obligatory; but the respective offices were already closed, effectively making me wait until Monday—with my car and luggage locked up in the customs shed!

Four days later, these obstacles had been overcome, but half the money my brother had wired me was also gone. To forestall any nasty surprises, I had my Beetle checked in Perth by an experienced mechanic from Berlin named Matscholl, who confirmed my suspicions: I had been driving in effect on two cylinders! Together we laboured all day, fixing everything properly. This good man then invited me to his home to eat and sleep—a real godsend!

By May 3, I was finally underway. I crossed the rabbit fence and reached Norseman, the last town until Port Augusta, to stock up for the trip through the desert. Driving along the unpaved Eyre Highway to traverse the two-thousand-kilometre Nullarbor Plain in 1962 was still considered quite an adventure. Water was available at the few tiny settlements, or "roadhouses," but there were next to no service stations or stores. Traffic on that often deeply rutted road was sparse and consisted of the odd supply truck; I saw no busses or passenger cars that week! Camping under the starlit skies and in total silence was great, as I enjoy feeling close to nature.

As always, I relied on the Lord, and He saw me through. Apart from two flats and an oil leak, I had no trouble reaching Adelaide. I called my brother when entering the State of Victoria, and soon found myself in the ACT (Australian Capital Territory), where Helmut came to meet me. The moment of which I had dreamt in darkest Africa had arrived: we met on the road between Yassi and Canberra with great joy, not unlike four years earlier, when we had met on the road, too, but in Tierra del Fuego at the tip of South America.

I was in Canberra almost three weeks. Thanks to Helmut's loan, I could book the return trip to Vancouver on the P&O liner *Oronsay*, and thus be back in time for my job and sundry duties. Before leaving, someone from the *Canberra Times* came to see me. The resulting interview and photo appeared on the front page in Australia's capital on June 17, 1962. Since the TV stations 2CA and 2CY had also got wind of the story, they both interviewed me. At the Canadian embassy, I had been told that this year I was the only one who had come from Canada with his car. That my journey had first led me across Africa was noted with considerable astonishment.

Incidentally, the trip across Australia from west to east—I would cross it from north to south twenty years later—comprised well over five thousand kilometres and took up half the five weeks I spent down under.

The return voyage from Sydney, with stops in New Zealand, Fiji, and Hawaii, was pleasant and, apart from crossing the equator and the dateline, uneventful.

In Vancouver, I was reunited with my wife and child, and after a long night drive we were back home on June 22, 1962. I had seen much of Australia, but my secret idea of perhaps relocating there never came about. The Lord had other plans for me.

The following year, our second daughter was born. Unfortunately, Karen would be the last child, as my wife was left alone at the critical time in the hospital, which turned her off forever from having more kids. This saddened me, but after our divorce years later I became the godfather of several Central American children and later still adopted my new wife's son.

The next years passed in a fashion typical for young families: we were fully occupied with bringing up the children and enlarging the house, with continuous money problems and loan payments. There was little time or money to go anywhere far on two-week holidays, but we lived in the scenic Kootenays and also visited the Rockies, which would impress anybody with the majesty of God's creation. Yet one year, in September 1964, I managed to drive up to Yellowknife at 62°N. Previously, from Fairbanks, I had booked a short flight to Fort Yukon, just beyond the Arctic Circle. However, the weather turned bad, and the eight-passenger Beechcraft didn't take off. The company offered to refund the tickets or fly the eight passengers on another plane. As I was the only one going for the latter option, I was flown there in a two-seater Cessna. And boy, were we tossed about in gusty winds, thunder, and lightning. It was quite scary. My guardian angel had a tough time, but he got us there and back.

The next year, my wife (who often felt homesick) flew to Germany with our kids for three months. In that time, I received word from Pater Myron, who had returned from the Congo to Montreal, that all his brother monks had been murdered by Simba rebels. The entire District of Paulis was in revolt with random killings—and I had driven through there alone. God had protected me! Yet the old question "why they, not I?" lingered on.

Entering Fairbanks Alaska, Jun 1959

Unloading my Beetle in Freetown, Sierra Leone, West-Africa, Jan 1962

Repairing my Beetle's engine in Bamako, Mali, Jan 1962

Hitch-hikers in Chad, Central Africa, Feb 1962

Lucky shot of a giraffe crossing the road in Queen Elizabeth Park, Uganda, Mar 1962

On the Equator, on the road to Kampala, Uganda, Mar 1962

Limping back to Nairobi, Kenya with a broken torsion bar, Mar 1962

The brothers meeting on the road nr Canberra, Australia, May 1962

Chapter Eleven
Once More (1966-67)

My brother had just returned from the Australian National University's first archaeological dig in Thailand, which was to be followed by others in the next few seasons. This was of great interest to me, especially as Helmut would soon be in charge of these Thai-British Archaeological Expeditions (TBAE). Being that I had not been to Asia yet, that I was fascinated by such digs, and that archaeologists can always use capable and cheap labour, I obtained a position as unpaid assistant from the leader, Professor Watson, provided I made my own way to and from the site. Thus the plan took shape to travel from the U.S. West Coast by freighter (with my car on it) directly to Thailand, meet with the TBAE members there, and drive together to the dig site. Afterwards everybody would return to their home country; in my case, by Beetle overland along the famous India-England route, and then by boat to Canada.

The question was of course whether I could afford that in terms of family, work, and money. I considered the constellation unique and a last chance: the kids were growing, and I was getting older, too. Besides, would I ever again be able to go on a real expedition, and with my brother at that? Ann would be happy to live in Vancouver with the MacKays (godparents of our daughters). At work, both my European supervisors supported the Asian venture, thus I was granted another six-month leave.

Money, however, was tight. My income went towards the house, my savings had evaporated when the finance company went bust, and I had to leave Ann with sufficient funds for the duration. My veteran Beetle—now eleven years old, with 240,000 kilometres on it—had been rejuvenated with an almost new engine recovered from a recently wrecked Beetle (a gift from God?) and would have to do once more. In fact, "Once more" became the new hood inscription, and indeed the motto for the whole venture.

For months, it was not even assured that it would take place at all. The universities involved needed to have the funds authorized first, whereas my preparations—notably bookings, visas, and vaccinations—had to be done well beforehand. There was much telegram traffic, with much at stake, until finally in October Helmut wired me: "Funds approved!" I managed to get space on the Pacific Far East Line's *Oregon Bear*, sailing from San Francisco to Bangkok on December 10, 1966. I would have to leave Trail four days earlier; Ann had already left with the children for Vancouver. This time I would soon be together with my brother, and the overland distances could not be worse than what I had faced in Africa four years earlier, so not to worry. Rather, I remembered Proverbs 3:5–6: *"Trust in the Lord with all your heart… and he will make straight your paths."*

Thus confident, I set out alone again on December 6, 1966 on my third and last world tour by car (there would be one more twenty years later, but by plane, boat, and train). The drive to San Francisco was uneventful but tiring, trying to make it on time. But as often happens with freighters, the departure was delayed for "at least three days," days I could spend with Jewish friends whom we had taken in earlier in B.C. They showed me blessed hospitality! My Beetle was loaded on the 13th, I was allowed on board on the 14th, and we finally put out to sea on the 15th, five days late. The *Oregon Bear* was almost twice as big and as fast as the lamentable *Del Monte* I had gone to Africa on, and it would be my home for seven weeks, together with seven other passengers.

We made good headway on a west-southwest course with little to see except albatrosses near the Midway Islands. We crossed the dateline (thus losing December 23), observed Christmas in pretty rough seas and cold weather, and then docked at Yokosuka, Japan. The ship also called at Pusan on New Year's Day, as well as at Sasebo and Nagasaki. After a stopover in Okinawa, we spent several days at Taiwanese harbours before steaming through the then-uneasy Formosa Strait, finally reaching San Fernando in the Philippines to unload cargo. Then we headed back to Okinawa to take military stores on board for the Vietnam War, which took four days. This gave me time to explore Naha and environs thoroughly, including the museum about the Battle of Okinawa (in which the entire Japanese garrison of a hundred thousand troops died). By that time, I had been on the freighter for a month and I was growing uneasy about getting to Bangkok to meet the TBAE members in time. We were told only that we would arrive on January 23, 1967, but would then face an uncertain wait in the lanes.

Sailing around South Vietnam, we "arrived" on the promised day, after some eleven thousand sea miles and thirty-eight days, only to drop anchor nearly twenty miles from shore, together with two dozen other ships. We remained there for another eleven days while my brother was waiting ashore—or so I thought; by that time, he had in fact already left for the expedition site.

On February 3, we actually docked in Bangkok harbour. The officials there were not exactly friendly, granting me only a fifteen-day visa and not letting my car on shore. Moreover, I was to leave the ship in the morning! Just as despair was raising its ugly head, the Lord helped again, this time by means of a letter with instructions, which my brother had wisely left with the shipping agency. This enabled me to call the Thai archaeologist at the National Museum and the Thai automobile club RAAT. After leaving several messages and going to their offices (by three-wheel mini-taxis), I did get the RAAT permit for my Beetle three days later. The museum assigned a Thai assistant to be my guide.

Frustratingly, that Thai assistant was "not available" for two more days; likewise, the customs chief let me dangle equally long, requiring a lot of forms and a hefty landing fee before releasing the Beetle (in which I slept at the pier, despite gawkers, noise, and mosquitoes). On February 9—fully sixteen days after arrival off-shore—I could finally leave Bangkok with its incredible traffic and left-hand driving. I picked up the assistant, and we drove via the old capital Ayuthaya to Lopburi, visiting some old pagodas and temples.

The temperature got hotter and the road worse; from Koke Samrong onward, it was so-called turtleback driving right up to our destination, Chai Badan, which we reached by evening. Shortly afterward, we found Bangalo Sri Pranakorn, the TBAE's lodging, where Helmut and I happily embraced. This was the highpoint of my already two-month-long tour! Little did we know that the low point would follow within days. C'est la vie!

I was introduced to Professor Watson, the English leader; a Thai archaeologist named Nikom Suthiragsa; and Dr. Parker, a New Zealand geologist before being familiarized with the situation. The excavation here would soon be completed. Helmut was then to explore another promising site at the northern tip of Thailand. Anyway, I had a place to stay and interesting work (plus meals). I had even become important thanks to my car, because the second expedition jeep had already dropped out. So we drove every day in a convoy of Austin Gypsy and VW Beetle to the dig site at Kok Charoen, which was very exciting for me—I was on a real expedition, and with my brother—a dream come true! We four foreigners functioned as supervisors for some twenty local workers who excavated and screened the soil within the surveyed squares. We also dug ourselves when anything like bits of bone, shards of clay, or other artefacts appeared.

We were dealing with a Neolithic burial site in which parts of skeletons estimated to be three thousand years old had been found, along with some pottery, the year before. My job was to watch that not even the smallest item was overlooked, to fix the position of artefacts encountered, to draw them exactly, and finish unearthing them myself. It is a peculiar feeling to expose ancient human bones. They make one think about life, death, and the transitory nature of it all.

Unfortunately, the work at this productive site had to be wound down due to the coming rainy season, and because Professor Watson had to leave. So we all worked full stretch despite the heat, as everything had to be surveyed, drawn, and packaged before the site could be covered up again. Since the other three had to leave for Bangkok, Helmut, Nikom, and I were to wrap up the dig and then proceed to Chang Saen, a good nine hundred kilometres north into the notorious "Golden Triangle," where Thailand, Burma, and Laos joined. My poor Beetle was now the expedition vehicle and had to carry not only my luggage, but also Helmut's equipment and Nikom's suitcase (he went by bus).

We started on Sunday and drove over washboard roads to Petchabun, then continued through banana plantations and palm groves to Phitsanulok for the night. The next day, we passed Sukhotai and Tak before reaching Lampang via a poor road with elephants pushing teak logs. On the third day, we climbed through tall woods to Ngao and Phayaok, where a sign caught my eye with the words "Marburg Mission." We went in and thus met friendly Mrs. Laufer, whose husband was pastor in Chiang Rai, our next destination. We could overnight there and then drive on past the junction to Burma (sixty kilometres distant) eastward to Chiang Saen on the Mekong River. This place was so remote and unsafe that we were promised a police officer for protection, but he didn't show up until the last day, so our personal guardian angels had to do the work!

Nonetheless, our reporting to the tiny Archaeology Office on February 15, 1967, turned into a personal catastrophe, inasmuch as we were handed two telegrams. One was from our father in Germany, informing us of the death of our dear mother by traffic accident on February 9; the other was from Professor Watson expressing sympathy, as he had received the news in Bangkok and forwarded it to us. We all (especially I, the youngest) had revered our mother and admired her selfless devotion and frugal lifestyle. Everybody had assumed she would outlive our father by many years. We were both extremely affected by the sad news, but being so far away, what could we do? Helmut and I quickly agreed to wrap up the TBAE as soon as possible and return to our respective home countries.

But first the dig had to be investigated. On the way there, over rough dirt roads, all of a sudden my car's gas cable broke, in the middle of bamboo jungle! While Helmut walked ahead to find a vehicle to tow us, an idea came to me—via my travel angel no doubt—to use the choke cable as gas cable. I could thus continue in a fashion with this hand throttle, until a kind of tractor actually came and towed us by moonlight back to Chiang Saen. What a day that was! After fitting my spare cable in the village smithy, we made our way to a Mr. Lek, on whose land two test squares had already been dug. Neither they nor two more we dug yielded anything, so we took ceremonial leave, putting off the work to the next season. With that, the expedition's work for the 1967 season had been completed.

We now had to return the thousand kilometres to Bangkok, from where Helmut would fly home to Australia. After dropping him off, I had to drive all the way to Singapore and take a boat to India, since the land route through Burma was closed. There was no time to waste, as the *California Mail* was supposed to sail on February 28. We set out on February 18, slept once more in the mission at Phayaok, and then continued back via Lampang to Tak. Afterwards it was a fast march directly to Bangkok, in great heat over dusty roads and savannah-like terrain. I would not want to drive that route again—through heavy traffic, at night, and on the left side of the road while dead-tired and often blinded. It's a wonder we made it without mishap, our angels having protected us. We rested in a hotel, then made our arrangements in the next two days. On February 23, our nice time together came to an end. I drove my brother to the airport, where we said goodbye—which again would be for a good many years.

Now I was alone again, and Helmut's departure and mother's death were sinking in. It was an effort not to remain downcast for long. The antidote was faith in God and purposeful activity! So I quickly drove to Nakhon Fathom and made the detour to the famous River Kwai. Next morning, I visited the Commonwealth cemetery where seven thousand Allied soldiers are buried. While that cemetery was well kept, the small Japanese one nearby appeared neglected. I couldn't dwell on these things, but had to go back to the main road heading south. I still had 2,500 kilometres to Singapore!

The drive down the isthmus to Chumphon, where the road to Malaysia splits in two, went through a picturesque region with palms and beaches, and also temperatures around 40°C! I swam in the Gulf of Siam, and later at Ranong in the Andaman Sea. Marvellous! Camping was no problem, but getting food was, so I had to dip into my reserves. Continuing on past Phuket, I made it to the border at Sadao on time and left Thailand after four eventful weeks. Entering Malaysia was fairly quick at sunset, forcing me to drive quite a ways in darkness, a risky matter given the left-side traffic, narrow roads, and few signs.

The next day, I made good time on paved roads through Ipoh and on to Kuala Lumpur. From there, I called the Everett Line in Singapore and learned that the *California Mail* was now not expected until March 6—a most annoying development, since time and money were tight. With my car serviced, I drove to Malacca and the house of well-off relatives of a man named Arul, who had shown me around Kuala Lumpur as he wanted to emigrate to Canada. It was a pleasant day with good Indian food, multilingual TV, and conversation.

On leaving Malacca, I drove in muggy weather to the Singapore junction and on to Johore Baru, to cross the strait in the morning. On March 4, I rode across the dam into Singapore—the southernmost point of this world tour, at 1°N—and I thanked the Lord for having let me reach this clean city-state without mishap. As I thought I had time, I also visited the Allied cemetery at Kranji, where 4,500 defenders of 1942 lay.

I struggled through heavy traffic to the city centre and the Everett agency, only to hear that my boat would not sail for another week! As luck would have it, the P&O steamer *Arcadia* was anchored in the harbour, and it was leaving for Bombay that very night. I took it as a sign from God; He helps those who help themselves, so up and at it! In wild dashes between Everett, the automobile club, customs, the passport office, and the bank, I managed to complete all paperwork in a few hours. I could now buy passage for myself and my car. I stood at the pier for loading by afternoon. With my last cash going for the stevedores, my Beetle was hoisted on board at about 6:00 p.m. I followed shortly afterwards, and half an hour later the *Arcadia* left port—surely a record! Thus I was underway and had saved myself several days of driving in India. God had probably figured I and my brave car could use a week's rest!

It was an enjoyable journey on this large and fast passenger ship with its British/Portuguese crew and Commonwealth passengers. We sailed up the Malacca Strait, across the Bay of Bengal, around Sri Lanka, and then up the west coast of India, docking at Bombay as scheduled on March 10. Now the serious travelling and fuss about my car would start again; secretly I envied the other passengers who would be in England in a couple of weeks or those who had booked the bus tour. I would have to master the same distance alone, the hard way.

Sure enough, I was tied up with red tape all afternoon, and when my car was finally unloaded and the carnet stamped, it was too late to pay the fees, for the office had closed. I watched the *Arcadia* leave port, then settled down for the night near the customs office. It was presumably safe there, but due to heat and truck traffic, I had no chance of sleep.

The next day, with the help of an Indian angel/agent, I paid the city and port fees, and by afternoon I had left the harbour area. By driving through the Gateway to India arch into the metropolis, the adventure of crossing West Asia and the Middle East had begun. Recalling Psalm 121:7—*"The Lord will keep you from all evil"*—gave me the necessary confidence.

It took me a good two hours to get out of this huge city of some ten million, with much wealth and even more poverty, only to find the same problems in Thane, a neighbouring industrial city with incredibly poor shanty quarters. Beyond it, the area opened up a bit, with many small towns and wild traffic compounded by oodles of holy cows and oxcarts hugging the middle of the road, not to mention the innumerable cyclists and even more pedestrians.

I reached Agra early one morning and thus had a good look at the famous Taj Mahal. There I also had the good fortune—international angel at work—to run into an English couple by the name of Gerrard on their way from Japan to Britain. We combined forces for the next two days, which simplified logistics and increased security, and so entered Delhi in a convoy. We took in the sights, did our shopping (always difficult alone), and arranged for our next visas; we did get them, despite the India-Pakistani tensions. At Ambala, with the Himalayas in the distance, we had to part, with the Gerrards heading for Kashmir and me for Pakistan.

I went straight for the Indian border town of Ferozepur, using my last rupees for gas and so-called chapatis (crackers with meat), of which I kept some for later. That was a bad idea. Processing at both sides went relatively quickly, but then I noted a western woman at my car: her name was Jane, and she was on her way to her fiancé in England from Australia. She had a large backpack, and absolutely wanted a lift. In view of my Beetle's condition, I didn't like the idea of additional weight, but I had to agree that she was vulnerable alone hereabouts. Besides, with a woman one is more likely to be considered harmless, so I let myself be persuaded and have never regretted it. My personal angel provided me with good company, if only for a couple of days.

I now drove with Jane on my cot and her backpack behind her in heavy hail to Lahore, then on to the capital of Islamabad where we met the Gerrards again, but we couldn't travel together as they wanted to stay awhile. On Good Friday, we crossed the mighty Indus and later, in continuous rain, passed through the historic Khyber Pass. By evening we reached the border with Afghanistan and were checked through efficiently on both sides.

From here on, one would drive on the right side again (for the first time since Thailand, and until Britain). Now my problem was that nowhere could any lodging or camping spot be found. Twice already we had been chased away, until we resignedly halted at the side of the road, tired and cold. The sharp temperature difference between India and Afghanistan had already given us the sniffles, and now—likely from spoiled meat in the chapatis—I became quite sick and very weak, though I was vaccinated against cholera. I also had mechanical and logistical worries, and few resources left. The next morning, I almost crashed into a checkpoint barrier near Jalalabad, which woke up the guards dozing nearby.

Everything was wet and cold, the road ascended to two thousand meters, and then it started to snow. Driving in those conditions was bad enough, but then I had a flat! Changing tires was no fun in my state of health. I also had to disappear several times into the bushes and would much sooner have rested.

At a viewpoint, God sent me help again in the form of a Mr. Wais from Kabul, who had studied in Germany. He invited us for tea and then to his home when he saw I wasn't well. This good man let us stay another day, and even took me to the bank and Iraqi consulate. We took a cheap hotel to rest a bit, then saddled up again after some grocery shopping. Driving on the new toll road from Ghazni to Kandahar along the Tarnak river valley was delightful. We passed through a mountain-ringed steppe with adobe villages and old fortifications, as well as camels here and there. We reached Kandahar in the late afternoon, found an affordable hotel, and enjoyed one last joint breakfast before separating. Jane's next destination was Herat, whereas mine was Quetta. I took Jane to the bus station, but as there were no seats left, I had to drop her off at the road junction where we said goodbye, wishing each other Godspeed.

Alone again, I drove southward through the desert, crossing into Pakistan a second time. The section to Quetta and then westward through Baluchistan to the Iranian border demanded much from both car and driver. It was a bare plateau with rocky outcrops and many stones, hardly any dwellings, and just the odd camel—and nothing more for the next two thousand kilometres! In that desolate area, and out of nowhere, I saw another Beetle coming. We both stopped and discovered that we were fellow Saxons, what joy! This was a dangerous region, if only because of heat, sandstorms, and remoteness. There were also no services of any kind anywhere.

On April 1, I entered Iran, and right at the border post I had to swallow anti-cholera capsules, even though I had been vaccinated in Canada. There had been an outbreak! The actual border formalities were dealt with just ahead of Zahedan without fuss, so I could sleep on the road to Bam.

Over the next few days, I struggled to make my way slowly over endless washboard and dirt roads through the lonely Lut Desert to Yazd, with some mechanical concerns and sand everywhere. As I wanted to see Persepolis in the worst way, I took the uncertain shortcut across the Zagros Mountains to access the highway to Shiraz—what a pleasure that was, for I finally drove on pavement after thousands of kilometres of bone-rattling washboard! After visiting the tomb of Cyrus the Great, I reached Persepolis that evening. Although partly destroyed by Alexander the Great in 330 B.C., the remaining structures are still most impressive; indeed, they are among the top cultural sites in the world.

I spent the night with some U.S. Peace Corps workers in Shiraz, had my car repaired in a makeshift fashion, went for another look at Persepolis, and then continued on to Isfahan, which boasts many famous mosques. Finally on a good highway, I could fairly speed to Tehran and the Canadian embassy to report in, pick up my mail, and seek advice. I decided on a quick detour to the Caspian Sea, but then via Baghdad and the main attractions of the Levant on the direct route to Germany and England, for my steamer would sail for Canada in five weeks!

First I worked my way up into the Elburz Mountains and over the pass down to the Caspian coast to Rasht (barely 150 kilometres from the border with the former U.S.S.R.), and then back via the Safid Dam to Quazvin. From there, via Ramadan and the Zagros Mountains, I reached Kermanshah, and after a cold night the border town of Quasra Shirin. There I had my car lubricated on the hoist, where they found to my chagrin that the frame head was cracked in several places. This was a serious matter, but no repairs were possible now. I had to be very careful and trust that the Lord would see me through.

After twelve days and 3,600 mostly difficult kilometres, I left Iran and entered Iraq at Khanaquin, where the border police were professional if a bit nervous: the Six-Day War would break out soon! Descending steeply into hot Mesopotamia—that is, the Tigris valley and Baghdad—I reached famous Babylon quickly. I visited the museum and toured the ruins extensively with the help of an Arab guide. It was moving for me to stand where Hammurabi governed, the Tower of Babel was built, and Alexander the Great died.

My next destination was Amman, thus I needed to backtrack a bit and take the state road to Ramadi and Jordan. There I had to submit to the most thorough inspection since the Congo: everything in the car and on me was searched! However, here the soldiers were professional in their appearance and their work. Generally at that time one fared well as an English-speaker, as the area was heavily anglophile.

Shortly afterwards, my speedometer cable broke. I installed the new one I had wisely taken along. I also changed oil at the side of the road—and was hit by a sandstorm while at it! When it abated, I was able to cross the Euphrates and fill up at Ramadi before tackling the thousand-kilometre desert stretch. But first another flat, again at the right rear; I had no trouble changing the wheel, but now had no spare left—guardian angel, take note!

The desert here is truly desert-like. Nothing but sand! With nothing to see, I continued briskly past Rutba and found myself in Jordan, though not officially. That didn't happen until the next morning at the border post at H-4 (an oil pumping station) and later at the army control point at H-5. Here, too, they were interested in my field glasses and camping knife, but after some banter with the guards I was allowed to keep them.

I continued towards Amman. An arduous drive through hilly terrain, several wadis, and narrow roads brought me to Wadi Musa, where one descends into Petra. This ruined rock city can only be accessed through the three-kilometre-long Siq Gorge, but it is worth the trip! I met a British and an American couple, and we five walked together through the amazing rock alleys of this historic place, then camped in our cars.

I really had to get a move on now and therefore skipped Aqabah and the Red Sea, barely two hundred kilometres away, taking instead the straight Desert Highway North. It was like in the movies: sand, sun, and camels. The direct road to Jerusalem was closed due to "manoeuvres," forcing me to detour via Salt and Jericho, which at that time, in spring of 1967, was still Jordanian territory, today's West Bank. I could thus make my pilgrimage to the holy sites without an Israeli visa—which I needed when I visited them again in 2009 with my wife. It must be an emotional high point for any believer to wander in Jerusalem's Old City, to see the Mount of Olives, the Garden of Gethsemane, and follow in Jesus' footsteps along the Via Dolorosa to His crucifixion site. They all left a deep impression on me, and brought Him and the Bible closer.

Then I turned around, first to the lowest point on earth at the Dead Sea, 394 metres below sea level, where I swam—or rather, floated. From there, I went to Jericho, likely the world's oldest still inhabited city. A little beyond there, I crossed the Jordan River near the site where Jesus was baptized, and from where the Mount of Temptation is also visible. In the evening, I walked around on Roman pavement in Jarash and admired the magnificent ruins there—always a reminder of how transient earthly glories are.

After entering Syria, I actually took the "road to Damascus," where Saul was converted. However, I didn't spend much time in the city itself, so as to have time to see Baalbek. I crossed into Lebanon with a transit visa and soon stood in Baalbek, the Heliopolis of the Greeks, which also contains the great Roman Jupiter temple—or rather, the famous ruins of six tall columns. Ancient history fascinates me, so I stayed for another look in the morning before returning to Syria to also take in the massive twelfth-century Crac de Chevaliers crusader castle; it was poignant for me, as an Officer in St. John (a Crusader Order going back to 1100 AD), as up to two thousand knights had once been stationed there.

As it was already April 20, I had to push on, notwithstanding the nasty weather through ancient Hamah and Aleppo. I left Syria without further ado. I was—and am—most grateful to the Lord that He let me see all these historic places I had long dreamt about.

After a fantastic ascent through narrow and winding roads, I caught sight of the Mediterranean at Iskenderun (the old Alexandretta). It offered a marvellous view after all that desert travel! Passing through a historic region with crusader castles to Tarsus (the birthplace of St. Paul), I reached Konya and continued through the Anatolian Plateau to the Aegean coast and Pergamum and its so-called acropolis. The entire stretch was quite picturesque, offering beautiful views and reminding one at every turn of many historic events, like at Troy and the Dardanelles, my last important stops along the way.

The site of Troy was somewhat disappointing. It was commercialized and poorly kept; nevertheless, it was important for any classical-minded person. Just think of Homer's Iliad or Schliemann's excavations!

At Canakkale, I had my Beetle's front-end welded in a so-so fashion. I also learned that insurance was required for entrance into Europe, obtainable only in Istanbul, meaning a time-consuming detour. So I took the ferry to the Gallipoli Peninsula the same evening, and was thus back in Europe!

Despite that emotional lift, I would need God's angels again. When I had the car lubricated, I cringed looking at it from below: it was much worse for wear! In addition, the political situation in Greece worried me, as the Colonels' Putch (the overthrow of the Greek monarchy) was underway there and threatened to result in border closings. The angels came through: I passed the Turkish-Greek border without problems, the way to Salonica was open, and I entered Macedonia the same evening.

The continuing rain was perhaps a hint to keep on driving; with good highways, me in a hurry, and little to see anyway, I made good time through the former Yugoslavia and Austria. After a quick flight to Madrid to see my dear pen pal Carmen again (for the last time, as she would die suddenly three years later), I could finally drive into Germany and head for little Einöd beyond Karlsruhe, where my sister Friederun lived with her large family. After great hellos, much happy talk, and some rest, we agreed on what to do next. With my GDR visa in hand (I had applied for it all the way back in Thailand) and space on my ship sailing from Liverpool to Montreal on May 16, I would travel to East Germany for five days of visiting relatives before heading for Bremerhaven and the ferry to England—provided, of course, the poor Beetle was still up for all that.

The border crossing went fairly well, and it was a strange feeling to drive through the home pastures after twenty years. Despite my late arrival, my father greeted me happily and wanted to hear the latest news right away. Widowed now, at seventy-four he still worked as director of Heine & Co in Leipzig. That company earned hard currency and he had excellent contacts, which is why he was kept on, later earning him the rare permit to move to the West.

With Father, we drove to downtown Leipzig for the mandatory police registration, and then to his office. I walked to the familiar places of my youth: the burned-out school, the bomb-damaged Luther church, and the parsonage. How many memories surfaced then—the school and confirmand periods, the night watches, my first girlfriend. Together, we continued to my sister Ki's now state-owned farm near Colditz, arriving late afternoon. Despite the shadow cast by Mother's death three months earlier, it turned into a wonderful meeting with her and all the family.

The next day, we went back home to Markkleeberg and laid a wreath at the family grave, where Mother's name had now been added to the headstone, beside Grandma and Walther. Afterwards we all said our heartfelt goodbyes and I drove back to West Germany, deep in thought.

I spent a day with my now-deceased godfather's daughter, and with godmother Ida and family. Both their places were out of the way, but these dear people had always been supportive of me. At the VW garage in Wunstorf, they shook their heads and told me that the frame head was beyond repair and that continuing would be risky—but what choice did I have? Pray, trust in the Lord, and carry on.

After dropping in on my parents-in-law near Rendsburg, I booked space on the Bremerhaven-Norwich ferry, and made it there just in time for loading onto the *Viking III*. The departure from Bremerhaven felt nostalgic. It was just as rainy and deserted as when I had emigrated from here sixteen years before.

After eighteen hours at sea, we anchored at Norwich and I felt relieved to be back in England. At Hampstead, I looked up my former Cominco chief, Dr. Campbell, who kindly arranged for me to stay at his father's house near Liverpool. Thus on May 16, 1967, I turned over my trusty Beetle to the stevedores. After driving eighteen thousand kilometres in ten weeks, this was its first rest since Bombay. I boarded the same *Empress of England* I had returned on from my first world tour. I gave sincere thanks to the Lord that my car and I had safely made it, and that I could at last sleep without fear.

The eight-day voyage, via Greenock/Glasgow and past Northern Ireland, was uneventful except for a gale the second night. The actual Atlantic crossing took only six days, and the sea calmed down. Yet I was concerned about the condition of my Beetle and whether I could make it back to British Columbia on time to resume work on May 30. We docked at Montreal on May 24—on Canadian soil again! I advised Volkswagen Canada in Toronto of my arrival there the next day, and drove those last six hundred kilometres carefully on good roads.

My car naturally caused considerable attention, for it was evident that it had travelled far and suffered much. The advertising chief, Mr.

Crocker—another angel—received me warmly, and then suggested, "You let us have the advertising rights, and in return we will buy your car and fly you home." As much as I hated to part with my faithful Beetle, under the circumstances it was the most reasonable solution, and I agreed.

The next two days included a whirlwind of interviews, pictures, and recordings with the advertising people, for which I received a few dollars and a free hotel. On my request, my car was inspected on the hoist by the VW master mechanic. Disbelieving, he told those present, justifying the sale, "In that one I wouldn't dare cross the street!" The official price was the airfare to British Columbia. Now I could phone my wife, still in Vancouver, and on May 27, 1967, I was back at my home in Rivervale near Trail, B.C. after an absence of six months and some sixty-three thousand kilometres by land and sea, with still a few dollars, but also with debts—and no car.

It was by no means easy to get back into the work and household routine, which many fathers of my generation will readily understand. Despite my job, reserve duties, and occasional translation jobs, the earnings were never enough, yet the house still required much work and the family more upkeep. In particular, a car was needed to go to work and do the shopping, and I soon found a neat 1964 Beetle. But all that, plus bank loans for the house addition and family contributions for car repair, had to be repaid.

We couldn't exactly live it up the next few years, but we did manage by the grace of God to live fairly contentedly—and in the beautiful surroundings of the interior of British Columbia.

The brothers meeting in Chai Badan, S Thailand, Feb 1967

*The Thai-British Archaeological Expedition team in Chai Badan:
L-R: Helmut, the author, Dr. Parker, Nikom, Prof Watson, Feb 1967*

In His Hands

Excavating a neolithic skull at Kok Charoen, Thailand, Feb 1967

Working elephants along the road in N Thailand; Helmut and my Beetle at right, Feb 1967

At the India-Pakistan border nr Ferozepur, Mar 1967

All alone in Baluchistan (Pakistan/Iran), Mar 1967

Partial view of the ruins of Persepolis, S Iran, Apr 1967

At the Iraq-Jordan border in the Syrian Desert, Apr 1967

At the world's lowest point by the Dead Sea (then Jordan) Apr 1967

Chapter Twelve
In Transition (1968–75)

One positive development was that more translation requests from Cominco engineers came my way. But these orders, tricky technical articles from German professional journals, were always urgent and poorly paid, so I often found myself sitting at the typewriter until late at night and feeling correspondingly tired the next morning. As time went by, I got better at it—and then came another hint from above, which would have astonishing consequences later. When I saw an ad in our paper, in which the federal government was looking for "freelance translators with a technical background," I applied. Soon after translating the required test text, I received the good news from Ottawa that I had been accepted! I now had one full-time and three part-time jobs, thus next to no free time. What little there was I spent working on the house.

Looking back, those were pretty good years. Canada was at its zenith at home and abroad, and the people celebrated the country's centennial in 1967 enthusiastically. The economy flourished, and by staying out of the Vietnam War, embracing peacekeeping missions, and liberalizing immigration, Canada gained much prestige. At the same time, West Germany suffered unrest and unemployment; nevertheless, Ann was sometimes homesick and tried to motivate me to return to Germany—she hailed from the West, I from the East, and Germany was still divided. But our daughters were Canadian by birth, both of us had been naturalized, and I served in the reserve army and worked part-time for the government. I considered our path set.

My world tours by Beetle produced an interesting sequel. After selling my trusty car to VW Canada, a lively correspondence developed between me, the VW sales staff, and their ad agency. As a result, my Beetle was exhibited in several cities in Ontario, notably at the popular Canadian National Exhibition in Toronto. That was topped by it being shown at the "Man and His World" Expo in Montreal for six months in 1968, together with some thirty of my photos. This netted me a dollar a day, a new set of tires, and a lot of mail which needed to be answered!

While I couldn't travel to Montreal myself, I was shown leaning against my Beetle on the inside cover of the '68 and '69 VW catalogues. I remained faithful to Volkswagen, soon exchanging my '64 Beetle for a '67 model, which I used until the end of 1980; it was my last Beetle, and my last car.

The winter of 1968–69 was until then the coldest and snowiest in the Kootenay District, with temperatures down to –35°C and 161 inches (over four meters) of snow! Due to the deep snow, I had to walk the seven kilometres to work several times and also shovel the snow off the roof to avoid collapse. With the spring came the dreaded flooding, which hit Trail particularly hard. This time, a creek flowing into the mighty Columbia was blocked by debris, forcing city and military engineers to blow a hole in the floodwall so the water could run into the river.

We engineer reservists had been called up over the radio for emergency service, to get our heavy trucks and equipment out of the armoury and then return downtown to rescue stranded people from the meter-high flood waters. As an experienced staff sergeant at the time, I was on duty nonstop for over twenty-four hours. Thank God, we were able to carry quite a few persons to safety without injury to our men— our personal angels had done it again! Incidentally, I visited Trail recently (in the summer of 2012) and noticed that those low-lying sections of town had been converted into a park; also, my beloved Rivervale house is no more.

Though I wasn't travelling around the world anymore, life was by no means dull. On the contrary, many changes came into my life, demonstrating God's wonderful ways. The world was mesmerized by the first man on the moon (July 1969), but for me personally the workload was of more pressing concern. Translation requests came from Cominco and the government at the same time, in addition to my regular job and reserve duties; just then, Ann went to hospital for leg surgery, requiring me to look after the kids.

Moreover, there were changes in the family: my eldest sister and family moved to Detmold, my brother completed another dig in Thailand, and my father finally retired at the age of seventy-five. What's more, he had met Hanni, a girlfriend of his youth, at the Leipzig Fair; both widowed now, they became friends again and decided to spend the rest of their lives together. Thanks to his rare GDR exit permit, he could move to Frankfurt to be with her. Father bequeathed the family home in Markkleeberg—in which I had been born and raised—to Ki and her husband; however, they had only trouble with it and ended up selling the property with a heavy heart (house ownership was frowned upon in the communist GDR).

Thus not only was the German family home lost, but now I also had to put up my beloved Rivervale property for sale, because a "real house" in trendy Warfield had become available when a colleague retired and moved away. Despite unfavourable conditions, to maintain domestic peace I gave in to Ann's urgings, and we moved there in 1970. I still worked evenings on translations in the now empty old house, as there was no office space in the new one. With Cominco falling on bad times, the Rivervale house didn't sell for a long time. Also Carmen, my pen pal of many years, died suddenly in Madrid at the age of thirty-seven. All in all, these were rather trying times, but I always remembered Romans 8:28—*"We know that all things work together for good for those who love God, who are called according to his purpose."*

Then the Lord helped again. Totally out of the blue, I received a query from the government in Ottawa late in 1970. Thanks to my good performance as part-time translator, they offered me a full-time position in the Translation Bureau—was I interested? Well, that looked like an opportunity for improvement—a public service career for me, big-city life for Ann, and better schooling for our girls! Ann came out in favour, and professionally the move was to my liking, as I couldn't advance any further at Cominco. Therefore I accepted the government offer, although I would thereby forfeit my pension rights from Cominco.

I first had to take a public service aptitude test, but it evidently went well, for the firm offer for a translator position came in mid-March. My position with the Foreign Languages Division started in early June. I gave notice to Cominco after almost twenty years and used my last holidays for a quick flight to Germany, both East and West. That way I could see both my sisters, father, and Hanni, as well as several family friends. Some of these good people I would not see again.

There was much to arrange, pack, and sort out, for first I had to drive alone in my car to Ottawa and send for the family later, once I had found accommodations. I converted my Beetle to a camper again and set out on June 1, 1971, across the Rockies and the Prairies to the boundary with Ontario. When I got out to take a photo of the marker, I was almost eaten alive by a swarm of pesky blackflies.

On another occasion, my guardian angel intervened. On the last night of this long trip, I camped as usual in my car in a clearing not far from North Bay. I woke up at dawn with a strange feeling, because the window on one side was dark—it was the belly of an upright black bear, investigating my roof carrier! When I sounded the horn, he ambled away.

I arrived in Ottawa as scheduled, found a hotel room, and presented myself on June 7 to the section chief, a Mr. Behne from Berlin. He showed me around and introduced me to my new colleagues—two Austrian ladies, two Germans, and an Englishman. I was placed in a room with two of the men, given a desk, a typewriter, some reference works, and the first big job right away!

I discovered quickly that here one was constantly kept on the go. There was plenty of work, and much of it urgent. The formerly little Translation Bureau, hitherto mainly concerned with immigrants' documents, grew rapidly after the Bilingualism Act of 1969 to some two thousand employees, now that all official reports had to appear in both English and French. The small Foreign Languages Division with its staff of about seventy (only half of them translators) had to tackle the orders for all other languages, also employing many so-called freelancers (of whom I had been one for three years). The FLD was organized into five sections: Romance, Slavonic, Germanic, Multilingual-into-English, and Multilingual-into-French, boasting some impressive linguistic genii.

My main concern now was to find a house for the family as soon as possible, yet advertised real estate prices were very high. Again the Lord helped me: a colleague drew my attention to a low-priced condominium subdivision under construction in Beacon Hill. I went there, looked at the hole where the house was to be built, and signed the contract on the spot! Alas, my troubles were not over. Construction was to be completed by August 10, but when my family arrived one week later, it was by no means ready to move in—not until the carpenters' strike was settled!

I had meanwhile rented a small attic room downtown, but was at a loss where to put up my wife and daughters. Here appeared an angel in the person of Miss McMunn from the Romance Section, who offered to share her large flat with my family for a couple of days—which stretched into twenty. We have not forgotten her kindness, though she died a few years later. By early September, we could at last move in and spread out. The new house had two storeys and a basement, plus a small yard and a parking spot.

Yet the debt load had become menacing. Though the old house in Rivervale had finally been sold (at a loss), the loan on the Warfield house and the previous owner's mortgage had to be added. For over a year I was paying three-quarters of my salary while my wife and children required more and more.

It was a tough period, as I had no additional sources of income. Thanks to God, little by little things sorted themselves out. My transfer to the Military Engineers in Ottawa came through, and not only that but this unit desperately needed another officer, and its commanding officer supported my renewed application so strongly that, after passing the aptitude and medical tests, I was "commissioned from the ranks" taking effect on September 15, 1972, although I was by then three years "too old"! Incidentally, to be accepted from an NCO (non-commissioned officer) rank to lieutenant was quite rare in the Engineers, but my new unit now had two who had taken the same path. The other one,

Lieutenant Pickworth, remains my best friend to this day; friendships lasting over decades are a real blessing.

The next few years brought normalization: I was secure in my job, the children did well in school, and we were active in church. Privately, it didn't look so good. Ann absolutely wanted to fly with the children to Germany (expensive for three), leaving me alone for two months. I had no holidays coming yet, though. Instead, my father and Hanni came to Canada in the fall to visit us. I was happy to pick them up in Montreal and drive them via Niagara Falls and colourful New York State to Ottawa. However, they soon noticed that not everything was well in our marriage. The new feminist movement was spreading in the 70s. A neighbour's wife had already left her husband (rare in those days), and Ann fell under the influence of similar-thinking women in the neighbourhood. She now went looking for work, and though I had agreed only to part-time work, she landed a full-time job at the Hudson's Bay Company. We now had the dreaded problem of so-called latchkey children, which I think may have contributed to troubles with our older daughter later.

I was too busy at the office, where we had so much work that we all had to put in a lot of unpaid overtime. The situation was similar in my Engineers unit, where we few officers all had double tasks to tackle, often until late at night. I couldn't effectively counteract the demise of my family life—at least I told myself that, or was it an excuse? A consolation of sorts was the fact that quite a few of my colleagues at work and in the military were in a similar fix, and consequently many long-standing marriages broke up. At any rate, in my opinion Women's Lib destroyed the traditional family as my generation knew it, or at least undermined it, without replacing that concept with anything better.

Meanwhile, I had passed the eight-month training period for new revisors at the Translation Bureau, and was then employed for many years as revisor/quality controller, responsible for the production of some forty freelancers. Besides my job, I was also taking courses to become a captain, mostly held at Camp Borden, which I reached by train. On the occasion of a railway strike, I hired a four-seater airplane—after all, God helps those who help themselves—in which we three little lieutenants landed directly on the parade square, causing some excitement (in typical military fashion, I was both reprimanded and praised afterwards). Later, I was still admitted to the major's course in Nanaimo, B.C., and I passed it well. Nonetheless, I was never promoted, as there was no position available. When in 1974 they were looking desperately for reservists to go on U.N. duty in Egypt, I volunteered and was accepted, but my section chief wouldn't let me go. In the following year, it would be my turn to go on the coveted German-Canadian translator exchange.

1975 would turn out to be a critical year. In the office, I had become deputy section chief and freelance administrator. I also held the position of security and first-aid officer on our large floor, as well as in my Engineers unit, where I was already plenty busy as training officer. In sum, I was overworked and falling behind in every area, without real holidays for years and without a comforting home life. Ann and I had drifted apart, and our daughters were left for hours to their own devices. In addition, I was the chauffeur for everybody, since I was the only one with a driver's licence. It was no fun driving in the ice and snow. That January, my guardian angel protected me from serious harm when I became involved in a typical winter car accident on Ottawa's busy Queensway in freezing rain. Two cars ahead of me started to skid and ended up sideways, blocking the lane. Despite all my defensive driving skills, bang! Luckily, there was only slight damage to my Beetle's body work.

In July, Ann flew briefly to Germany and returned just before I was due to leave for the German Federal Language Office near Cologne. She had said something about leaving me if I didn't mend my ways, which I didn't take seriously enough.

The three months on exchange were most rewarding professionally, militarily (I was also there in my capacity as a Canadian captain), and privately, as I could visit my father and sister as well as take part in some weekend excursions. Most memorable was my visit to the German Navy monument at Laboe in honour of the thirty-five thousand sailors who perished in the First World War, and the 120,000 (including thirty thousand in submarines) of the Second—more than the entire Canadian Forces at the time! A walk through U-995, moored there, brought back memories of my day on a training sub in the Baltic in 1943. After tacking on one week of holidays exploring the island of Mallorca, I returned to Ottawa on November 20, 1975.

The Lord then threw a spanner in the works, and it took me a long time to see any good in it. After some unpleasant days, Ann told me she would leave me, and I was to explain the separation to our daughters, then twelve and fourteen! Brigit, the older of the two, stated she would go with her mother, and Karen said diplomatically, "I go where my sister goes!" I was thus embarrassingly isolated in my own home. It was of course difficult to have one's mind on the job when domestic peace had been shattered. When I was called a few days later by Ann's lawyer, I sat there so dumbfounded that my chief gave me the rest of the day off. The next day, the military transferred me—with excellent timing—to Militia Headquarters, where one obviously had to pull oneself together, which helped.

On returning home from work on December 10, I noticed a moving van on our street, yet none of the neighbours had said anything about plans to move. Then I could see that it was my house being emptied! Ann had just moved with the children into an apartment block nearby, evidently prepared well beforehand. I even saw them walking away, for the actual move had been delayed. Ann was able to call out to me to meet them in half an hour at the corner restaurant for one last supper together. Well, afterwards they all went quickly to their new apartment, and I sat alone in an empty house with a heavy head. I was in a fine mess!

The faithful Beetle exhibited in the German Pavillion at the 1968 "Man and His World" Expo in Montreal

The family in Ottawa, ON, June 1973
L-R: Anneliese, Brigit, the author, Karen

Brake trouble nr Veracruz, Mexico, Apr 1979

Dialogue with a kangaroo, Katherine Gorge NP, Northern Australia, Mar 1981

Chapter Thirteen
Back to Central America (1976–82)

Two weeks after my wife and children moved out, it was Christmas, the feast of love, yet it turned out rather gloomy. I could visit my daughters briefly, but it felt strange. Well, many have had to go through similar tribulations, so I don't have to dwell on what goes on inside a broken family. It was bad enough that my wife of fifteen years had left, but the children, too! The only legal way to get them back would be by court order; likewise, the payments I made to Ann to tide them over weren't recognized, as they had not yet been stipulated by contract.

After months of unpleasant negotiations, the separation agreement was signed in May 1976. Back then, three years had to pass before either side could file for divorce; I wore my wedding band until the final divorce decree in April 1980. These months and years were a time of self-examination. Had I failed as a husband and father or was I a victim of the social changes of that period, or both? Though it was still a stigma in our circles, all my family proved true friends in my predicament, providing mutual support that has continued among us all those years. My task was to adapt to the new situation, maintain contact with my daughters, and get a handle on the money situation. To avoid brooding, I dove into work both at the Translation Bureau and at Militia Headquarters.

Yet *"we know that all things work together for good to them who love God"* (Romans 8:28). Slowly I could see God's plan to make me a better person, more concerned about others. I thought long and hard about mankind in general and human relations in particular, and came to the conclusion that only the latter really matter in life—that is, more than position, rank, income, and possessions—as is written in the Bible. From this realization, reinforced by earlier religious and parental teachings, it was only a small step to becoming more socially engaged instead of bemoaning one's own misfortune. I had been a frequent Red Cross blood donor for many years already, but when I heard of a Canadian organization for foster children in Central America called Horizons of Friendship (formerly HHF), which was affiliated with SOS Children's Villages International, I told myself, "Here you can do some good, for there is no hope of more kids of your own."

One year after our separation, I became the "godfather" of a ten-year-old girl in Nicaragua, who was followed over the years by eight more (including one boy), often two or three at the same time, and all able to write. I have maintained a lively correspondence with all of them (which helped improve my Spanish) and visited each one, some several times. One, an orphan named Marisol in El Salvador, grew especially close to me, and I have supported her for over twenty years.

In 1977, I was made Officer-in-Charge of Cartier Square Armoury in Ottawa, and as such I also had to allocate rooms to qualified organizations. As I accommodated the St. John Ambulance Brigade several times, I was soon asked to join their staff, and I have remained an active member for many years.

I saw God's hand in all this only much later. My years as a volunteer first-aider have given me considerable practical experience and, coupled with knowledge of Spanish, equipped me well for work in the medical ministry—my main volunteer activity for the last thirty-five years—which in turn often enabled me to visit one or more of my foster children when working in their respective country.

However, given my daily work at the Translation Bureau, two evenings per week and some weekends at Headquarters, and now the training sessions and many duty hours at St. John Ambulance, I was fully occupied, not to mention correspondence, household, and family concerns. These latter involved not only money, but also my daughters, who were teenagers—a difficult time for all.

At work, we had been moved to Hull, on the Quebec side of the Ottawa River, for political reasons. The separatists had gained power there, and the federal government wanted to make its presence felt using several thousand civil servants. It was an unpopular move, as virtually all of us lived on the Ontario side and now had a longer commute. Moreover, we were put into so-called open offices—quite unsuited for mental work like translating or revising. Three of our staff quit, putting additional strain on the remainder. I had to stand in for the chief several times, putting in many extra hours; I felt physically down and inwardly alone.

As my father's eighty-fifth birthday and Hanni's seventy-fifth fell close together, they had the nice idea of celebrating them jointly in a big way, Father's last logistic effort. Thus a great family feast took place in Königstein in May 1978. Friederun was present with her husband and three of her children, I had come from Canada with my daughters (with Ann's permission), Helmut sent a telegram from Australia, but Ki wasn't allowed out of the GDR; all others were from Hanni's side. We soon had to fly home again, and I clearly remember that farewell from my father; when I said "Auf Wiedersehen" (meaning "until I see you again"), he replied, "My dear son, that won't be." Six months later, he died from a heart attack.

Thus we four remaining siblings were suddenly the "old ones," yet even though the cohesion among us remained strong, we were cut off from each other—Friederun in West Germany, Ki in East Germany, Helmut in Australia, and I in Canada. Not easy to meet for tea!

That fall, I was transferred for six months to NDHQ/DGIS (National Defence Headquarters/Director-General Intelligence and Security) in my capacity as both revisor and officer, in order to shape up the translation section there, which I managed to do. The sympathetic colonel approved a special bereavement leave for me to attend my father's funeral in Detmold, whereas the communist authorities again denied my sister Ki's request to take part.

I had no social life and at that stage didn't want one. The occasional mess dinner was enough for me, and the uniform was my only formal dress. When my daughter Brigit was eighteen, she was returned to me; nevertheless, due to her unsettled lifestyle, she forfeited her last year at high school and later lived with friends, becoming semi-independent. But the Lord helped her back. Eventually she graduated very nicely and overcame her problems. Karen had graduated with honours earlier and studied at the University of Victoria; both now have steady jobs and relationships.

1979 had been declared the "Year of the Child." I used that occasion to drive to Nicaragua to visit my foster-child Yadira in the SOS Village of Estelí. My 1967 Beetle, with over a hundred thousand kilometres under its belt, and the twenty-year-old equipment of my world tours, had to serve again. Gas was still cheap, but some Central American roads would be a challenge, likewise the revolutionist troubles at my destination. I wrangled a one-month holiday and left in mid-April, relying on my international angel to be on guard.

I made good time to Central Mexico, the only trouble being that the car's top wasn't watertight anymore: I had to wipe it dry inside after every rainfall. Also, the rusty mounting of the rear bumper shook itself loose; all attempts to fix that failed, forcing me to take it off altogether (earning a ticket from a U.S. highway patrol on my return).

Once in the hilly country of Veracruz, I noticed to my dismay that I couldn't brake well. The front left brake drum had seized! Besides, the engine pinked, protesting the poor gasoline and great heat. I had to stop at the edge of the road and dismantle the wheel; I was able to free the drum, but the brake was gone. I carried on carefully, still managing a good visit to the Mayan ruins at Palenque and daring the shortcut to San Cristobal before limping into Quetzaltenango to have the brake fixed. Thank heavens! Upon my arrival, I was introduced to a Mayan girl named Silvia, whom I subsequently accepted as my second foster child.

Getting to Honduras required fording a river near Chiquimula, because the bridge had broken down. With quick prayers and deft steering I made it across in my "amphibious" Beetle, to the astonishment of bystanders! In the SOS Village of Choloma, I picked up a Canadian social worker displaced from Estelí as guide. To be on the safe side, we gave a lift to an old hitchhiker, although my cot wasn't designed for two extra people and their luggage.

Eventually we were allowed into Nicaragua, and after a tough drive in darkness and fog we made Estelí late that night. The director and the house-mother presented shy Yadira (then twelve) to me. The next day, we spent some happy hours with the other children. As the first foreign visitor, I was a sensation; I was driven through the partly shot-up city centre, and then sent off with a serenade. It was deemed too risky to stay. Therefore I left the same night, got out all right, and didn't sleep until I had reached Honduras. My guardian angel also saw me safely through El Salvador (on the brink of civil war) to Sonsonate, where I met with Father Flavian, who had founded the SOS Village there and now headed the Agape Project, which I have also supported for many years.

With my tour of four SOS Villages in as many countries completed, I now had to get back to Ottawa in twelve days!

Crossing Guatemala, with another stop at Quetzaltenango along the Ruta Pacifica, and getting into Mexico was no problem until Tehuantepec, from where I intended to take the coastal road to Acapulco (then still a small town) before turning north. Unfortunately, the entire stretch to Pochutla was still under construction or not even begun yet. For hours I continued in first gear, through tight curves on narrow dirt roads and across several creeks. The poor Beetle had to work hard but carried the day, and I camped rather relieved near Puerto Escondido.

After passing through the aptly named Infernillo (meaning "little hell") to Uruapán, the next three days saw me laboriously making my way to San Luis Potosí, from where the good highway took me rapidly via Saltillo to the border and back into Texas, where I could finally stretch out. As I was driving through Illinois, a red warning light came on—the car's generator wasn't charging and wouldn't last long! Here the Lord threw me a life-saver in Wilhelm, a son of my godmother Ida, who had moved near Milwaukee. He escorted me to his home, and while my car was being fixed, I rested up for the night ferry across Lake Michigan. That way I could cross via Sarnia into Canada, drive through dense traffic to Toronto, and stay at friends near Peterborough. The next day, I stopped at Cobourg (the office of then HHF) to report and then carry on to Ottawa, arriving on time and greeted by my daughters.

With God's help, I had completed this last journey, which hadn't been easy on the twelve-year-old Beetle and fifty-year-old driver. After all, the distance of sixteen thousand kilometres had to be covered in thirty days, often in great heat, sometimes on bad roads, and under civil-war-like conditions in two countries—the international angel had done a good job! Travelling on a shoestring, I had managed not only to visit my two foster children, but also to obtain direct insight into life and poverty in the real Central America, my "sphere of interest" where I would spend much time later (and into which I would marry). I should also admit that this kind of forced march took a greater toll of me now than it had twenty years earlier.

Now came several blows. No sooner had I settled into my daily routine than I was served with the divorce petition, against which I raised no objection. As the court sat only a few times a year, the matter dragged on until January 1980, when a provisional decree was issued, leaving a three-month reconciliation period open. As I still lived in the family townhouse and Brigit was again with me (she had tried living elsewhere), I let it be known that there was a chance for a new start. Alas, it was not to be, and the divorce became final in April—it was all over.

Those were also difficult times for my ex and the children, notably Brigit. However, the family ties remained strong and eventually everybody found their feet again. Still, that time was hard on me, given that I was already overloaded at work and with other duties. Also, my sister Ki had had a relapse in East Germany, putting her continued existence there at risk.

My foster children, the Agape Project, and charity work in general took up an ever greater part of my private life. At the Red Cross, I made my seventy-fifth donation, and in the Engineers I completed my last summer exercise, my position at Militia Headquarters being extended once more. At the Translation Bureau, we had a strike that fall which, though settled in two weeks, only worsened the work climate.

All the foregoing stress and worry combined to put me into a poor state of health, and soon into hospital. There I had to undergo an unpleasant procedure, and the effects of it and the general anaesthesia bothered me for weeks afterwards.

However, the Lord also provided a happy antidote: my travel agency had a special offer for an affordable bus tour crossing Australia from north to south, which required an immediate decision. After calling my brother in Canberra and being invited to see him, too, I acted quickly and bought the tickets. In mid-March 1981, I flew to Sydney, still a bit shaky, where Helmut came to meet me. After twenty years, I was in Australia again! This time I didn't have to drive myself, since I was on a two-week camping tour by bus from Darwin to Melbourne. I was able to add another three weeks, to spend time with my brother's family and also gain an impression of the South Pacific region.

While I had left Ottawa amidst snow flurries, it turned quite warm in Brisbane and hot in Darwin, where the twenty-odd passengers gathered. The bus was a solid vehicle, with a kangaroo shield in front and a trailer with camp beds and folding chairs behind. We drove first to Kakadu National Park and then to Katherine Gorge. There we had to wait in 40°C heat for a spare part, and then another day because an older passenger had gone missing. As it turned out, he had wandered into a patch of elephant grass—and died there of heat stroke!

The long ride through the barren Northern Territory became interesting at the Devil's Marbles, and the next day we got to Alice Springs, in the centre of Australia, where we all went for a camel ride. From there we visited the imposing Finks Crevasse and Ormiston Gorge by sunset. I ran back to take a picture before dark, but got stuck in a rock cleft, spraining my foot rather badly, the guardian angel having prevented worse. I didn't mention anything for fear of being sent home, but the next day everybody noticed my swollen foot. Fortunately, they let me limp along, so I could see the amazing Ayer's Rock and the opal mines at Coober Pedy in South Australia before reaching Melbourne, the end of the tour.

I took the ferry to Devonport, explored Tasmania for three days by rental car, and returned to Melbourne by plane. From there, I took an express bus to Canberra and had a wonderful week with my brother and family. Then it was off across the Pacific to the Cook Islands, where I had booked a cabin on Roratonga, for glorious walking and swimming. I also hopped aboard a small plane to Aitutaki atoll and enjoyed a marvellous day at the palm-fringed beach in crystal-clear waters.

Unfortunately, my stay in this dream world quickly came to its end with a return flight via Tahiti and Los Angeles to cool Ottawa, just in time for Easter.

In Ottawa, I faced the old trot again, but soon movement came into my life. In May 1981, my chief handed over the section to me, quite exhausted after nine years on that demanding job. That was somewhat ironic, as I myself was quite run-down, and I had no idea then that this short-term appointment as interim chief would last almost a year! Meanwhile, I had passed the Health Ministry's first aid instructor's course and thus became the official "medicine man" on our floor. I had also accepted a third foster child, ten-year-old Marisol in Sonsonate, El Salvador. She would become my closest and longest-lasting one. In addition, I continued taking part in Ottawa's Miles for Millions charity marches (now thirty-five kilometres) and enjoyed long bicycle rides on nice weekends. While biking, I conceived the idea of visiting my foster children in their somewhat remote SOS Villages in Central America by bicycle, and I did exactly that the following year.

In the meantime, my daughters (now twenty and eighteen) and I went on another real camping tour—complete with tent and camp fires—in the Rockies in early September, as it would be progressively more difficult to do that later in our lives. We flew to Calgary, where I rented a car. We toured Banff, Jasper, and Yoho National Parks, hiked at several locations, and marvelled at God's creation. We also made a swing through the scenic Kootenays, into the familiar area around Trail, B.C. and Rivervale, where my daughters had spent their childhood, and to the now-closed HB Mine, where I had worked thirty years earlier.

After that enjoyable week, which brought the three of us even closer, I had to go right back into the thick of it. The chief remained burnt-out and abdicated, forcing me to stay on as interim chief besides my regular work, military, and St. John duties, a combination that couldn't go on much longer. And it did not. The position was filled in March

1982. When handing over the chief's duties, I suffered a real collapse—but my guardian angel made me wake up in the emergency room of our office tower by afternoon, to the relief of all involved.

At last I could take a month of holidays and carry out the bicycle tour to visit my three foster children in Central America. This was no doubt a rather audacious undertaking, given my still below-par state of health, the political strife in two of the four countries, unknown terrain, and hot climate. This called for my international guardian angels to be on "high alert," as my daughters put it. I had written to the four SOS Villages of Choloma, Estelí, Sonsonate, and Quetzaltenango, then obtained the four visas necessary and prepared my three-speed bicycle accordingly with a breadbasket, saddle bags, blanket, and repair kit, as well as two water bottles clipped to the frame. There was neither time nor opportunity for training. In late March there was still snow on the ground in Ottawa, and it was too cold for biking.

Under light snowfall, I loaded my bike onto the plane bound for Miami and then San Pedro Sula, Honduras, where I arrived in 30°C heat. The short ride to Choloma was useful to acclimatize myself and check out the equipment; everything worked fine, and I reached the SOS Village at suppertime. The director showed me around the village with its two hundred fifty children (including refugees from Nicaragua), and after a day of rest he took me and my bike in his van quite a ways towards the capital, Tegucigalpa, which I entered the next morning. At the National SOS Office, Doña Myrna greeted me warmly and also approved my plan of heading for the other Villages, each about five hundred kilometres apart, and with each telephoning ahead to the next one. That way I could always count on a bed and meal after several tough days riding and risky nights sleeping in the open.

First I had to pedal two full days through hot southeastern Honduras and cross the war-torn bridge near Ocotal into Nicaragua to get to Estelí. There they showed me around the village and fetched Verónica, a dark girl of fourteen, my new charge. Regrettably, I had to push on the next day, because the tense political situation made any border crossing uncertain. Yet all went well, the border guards being astonished to see a lone cyclist.

The ride through southern Honduras to the border with El Salvador was very strenuous, if only due to the heat. Once I was so bushed that I had to rest, but on that treeless route there was no shade anywhere. Finally I saw a dried-up bush, dragged my bike under it, and dozed off. When I got up later to ride again, I discovered a long thorn in the rear tire! I had to mount my spare tube, and in that heat! In addition, the country was torn by civil war and a curfew was in effect, therefore I could not camp in the open.

I had made it into El Salvador at Amatillo and was now near La Unión, wondering where to sleep. There the Lord helped me again with an angel in the form of a man who recognized the SOS Children's Villages flag on my bike. He waved me into his yard and let me sleep in his hammock. He also gave me a ride on his tanker truck for quite a distance (and passing two dead soldiers), so that I reached Sonsonate the following night, sunburnt and hungry. Pater Flavian, who remembered me from my previous visit by car, could hardly believe that I had made it unharmed. We celebrated the tenth anniversary of this SOS Village, but for me the high point was seeing little Marisol again, the brightest among my foster children. After visiting the huge Agape Project in nearby Izalco and meeting with Mrs. Sinnhuber, the SOS Director for Central America, I had to leave the next day. The goodbyes were difficult, and they were followed by a joint ride to near the border, where I was left alone again.

Southern Guatemala is a paradise of tropical fruits, so the long ride westward was quite tolerable. But then began the steep ascent to Quetzaltenango, over 2,300 metres high. Hard work! When I arrived at the SOS Village there, I ran into my Silvia, now a slim fifteen-year-old who recognized me and hugged me right away. I rested here for a day and also took in the Good Friday procession, which was quite unique.

On the director's advice, I pedalled along the Ruta Pacifica again, as the northern route was considered unsafe. By now I was well-trained and thus reached Guatemala City two days later, resting up in Mrs. Sinnhuber's office for the last lap into Honduras. I crossed the border near Copán, visited the famous Mayan ruins there extensively, and continued to San Pedro Sula, and from there in triumph to my starting point, Choloma, on April 15, 1982. The next morning, Don Sergio drove me and my bike to the airport, and by late evening I was back in Ottawa, to the joy of my daughters.

With the help of the Lord, His international angels, and some good people, I had realized my program of visiting my three foster daughters in Central America by bicycle. I had covered some 2,500 kilometres and (temporarily) lost fifteen pounds—all that on the cheap, often camping outdoors and on muscle power, at age fifty-three.

With my daughters in the Columbia Icefields, Jasper NP, Sep 1981

Taking a break on my Central-American bicycle tour, near the Guatemala-Honduras border, Apr 1982

Chapter Fourteen
Studies, Medical Missions, and the
Trans-Siberian Express (1983-88)

When I returned to duty at Militia District Headquarters, I was informed that, in accordance with a new directive, all reserve officers over fifty were to be discharged immediately—and that included me, now in my third extension.

After twenty-seven years, I now found myself with two evenings and several weekends available. As I had felt a need to upgrade my education for quite a while, now appeared to be the time to apply to university in Ottawa. While I was accepted, it would have meant evening classes, for which my chief wouldn't give me the extra hour off: "Not in the contract!" Fortunately, my angel made me see an ad by the University of Waterloo, whose correspondence program was leading at the time. I was accepted, on the basis of my good "Abitur" (college entrance exam back in Germany) and a few other classes, for the second year of Environmental Studies, majoring in Geography, and could thus start in the spring of 1983. It was a daring undertaking to attempt thirty-five years after high school, with a demanding full-time job plus St. John duties and much correspondence. On the other hand, my failed marriage still had the effect of giving me little desire for a so-called social life. On the contrary, throwing myself into academic work seemed a good antidote.

The next six years—during which I pursued two bachelor degrees, a Bachelor of Environmental Studies, graduating in 1986, and a Bachelor of Science, graduating in 1989—were characterized by so much work and study that there was little time for anything else. True, some other things crowded in as well. At work, the procedure for employing freelance translators—my responsibility—was totally revamped. The new contractors came under a centralized French-speaking agency, which spelled trouble for our Multilingual Division. Also, my daughter Karen moved to Victoria and studied at UVic. This led to several visits on my part, culminating in the purchase of a house there, as I aimed to retire to B.C. eventually. I was also involved in frequent correspondence with my Central American foster daughters. Spanish culture and language, as well as Meso-American history, would become lifelong hobbies for me—with remarkable consequences.

At about that time, I read an article in the September 1982 issue of *Reader's Digest* about a medical group from Canada which had performed eye surgeries and distributed glasses to the poor in Nicaragua for two weeks. They also employed helpers, which caught my attention, because similar organizations (notably Doctors Without Borders) accepted only health professionals and for longer terms. Being somewhat attuned to medicine myself—my mother had been a nurse in WWI, and I served in St. John Ambulance and the Red Cross—I inquired with the organization, known at the time as EMAS, then MGM, and later MMI: Medical Ministry International of Hamilton, Ontario. I was accepted initially as a repairman, and after a few missions and Spanish courses as an interpreter, in which capacity I have served ever since.

On my trimester holidays in July 1984, I went out with such a medical team to Yoro in Honduras. Although conditions were quite primitive, this charitable work appealed to me, as one was among similar-minded people and could practice Christian living. Despite the cost—one pays the airfare plus a project fee and receives no pay, only a tax benefit—this activity suited me rather well, for I could gain practical knowledge in medicine and in Spanish, and "for free."

I managed to go on such medical missions each July for the next six years, always to Honduras. After my second graduation—the Lord had sent angels to keep me going, for near the end of the Bachelor of Science program I was exhausted—and especially after my early retirement, these missions became my main occupation and expense. Indeed, I have derived much satisfaction from the work and felt good doing it. Though I'm neither a trained pastor nor a medical doctor, I can dabble in both their activities and encourage the often worried people. On "retiring" in 2015, I had served on over a hundred such missions in Latin America, most of the time interpreting between patients and doctors, and thus have probably talked to about thirty thousand patients. I have also been able to combine several mission trips with visiting one or more of my foster children in Central America, once (in 1987) all three. Thus the medical missions became the main component in my triad of medical work, foster children, and Spanish language, as well as the catalyst for my later marriage.

However, it wasn't always smooth sailing on those medical missions, directed as they were to the poor in the third world and so were inherently risky in regard to health and safety. On my third mission in 1986, to the interior of Honduras, I had my first close call, requiring divine intervention. I was with the advance party travelling in a jeep from Yoro to a remote village called Quebrada. While we set up shop and were waiting for the main team to arrive, I felt faint and slid down. The lone nurse in our party slapped me, trying to coax coherent answers out of me. Failing that, she stuck a note "heart attack" on me (as I heard later) and had me driven all the way back to Yoro and the little hospital where our doctors worked. They determined that I had suffered from heat stroke and very high fever. Thanks to my guardian angel and the treatment (cold bath, lots of IV fluids), I recovered over the next two days. Their public hospitals provide a bed and treatment, nothing else. Sheets and meals are a matter for the patient's family. In my case, a sister of the convent near where we were billeted kindly looked after these needs.

On completion of my first bachelor degree in October 1986, I treated myself by flying to Germany, because my brother had come from Australia, and my sister Ki, a pensioner now, had finally received permission to make a visit to the West! We brothers could thus meet with her at our eldest sister's place in Detmold. This was the first and last time we remaining four siblings were together. Ki died two years later, in February 1988. But she could at last freely tell us about her three years in the Soviet-run "special camp," where she had been held on an illegal weapon possession charge. Under the communist regime, all released prisoners were obliged to maintain strict silence. She also related a conversation with a flying buddy of our fallen brother Walther, according to whom many a comrade had chosen, faced with the hopeless situation, to sacrifice himself in suicide missions. We will never know the exact circumstances of his plane crash.

Meanwhile, I had piled up a lot of overtime at my government job at the Translation Bureau, because we were drowning in work due to the 1987 decision to really go after any remaining war criminals. As the only one in the office who could still read the archaic Gothic script of many German documents, I was heavily involved in that onslaught and soon became exhausted. I asked for and got three weeks off in September 1988, and decided to use them for a trip on the famous Trans-Siberian Railway, something I had always wanted to do. This would turn into another around-the-world trip, but this time without a car, just using public transport.

I obtained the necessary Soviet documents through an agency in Ottawa. They weren't easy to get for single travellers even then, barely three years before the U.S.S.R.'s demise. I had to prepay most everything, and at reasonable prices. The plan was to journey by plane to Tokyo, by boat to Nakhodka, by train to Moscow, by plane to Volgograd and back, then by train to Berlin and Amsterdam (via Leipzig and Detmold) for the return flight to Ottawa. And that is how it went, with my international guardian angels evidently on duty and looking after me, especially near the end.

On August 26, 1988, I flew from Ottawa to Vancouver (with a stopover in Edmonton, to look up my niece), followed by an eleven-hour flight to Tokyo and a bus ride to Yokohama. The next day, I boarded the new Soviet ferry *Konstantin Chernenko*, built in Stettin in 1986—at 12,800 tons, it was the same size as the refugee ship I had come to Canada on in 1951. She was certainly designed for hundreds of passengers, but on that morning barely thirty-five persons gathered for the two-day voyage across the Sea of Japan to Nakhodka, some one hundred kilometres east of Vladivostok (which then was a Soviet Navy base and therefore off-limits). The inspection was carried out by Soviet soldiers, not customs people, and rather roughly at that. They insisted on seeing my suitcase, simply not believing that I was travelling merely with a shoulder bag. They were equally particular about the currency declaration.

Therefore, it took a long time before we few people were taken to the train station and the Vostok Express. On it, we rode along the Ussuri River—the border with the People's Republic of China—to Khabarovsk, where the next day we switched onto the actual Trans-Siberian Express, named *Rossija* (Russia). The train consisted of two powerful diesel-electric locomotives and a dozen carriages, all built in East Germany. I was again in a second-class sleeping car compartment for four, which would be my home for a full week.

With me in the compartment were two young Hungarians and the girlfriend of one of them. In the evening, we three men went outside for a while to allow her to prepare for bed. The couple had the upper beds, which were folded during the day against the wall; bedding had to be drawn for a fee from the "provodnika," a mighty woman who not only kept the car clean and made tea in the samovar, but also guarded the passport of any foreigner who wanted to stretch his legs at a stop.

Normally the train stopped every two or three hours, but only for a few minutes, so as to maintain an average speed of sixty kilometres per hour overall. The whole system went by Moscow time, though the route passed through six time zones. The simple toilets were locked ten minutes before and after stops to keep the stations clean. On the platforms, one could buy fresh vegetables, yoghurt and such, even without knowing the language. In our compartment, we conversed in a mixture of German, English, and bits of Russian (among themselves, they spoke Magyar). I had a Russian phrase book with me, which came in handy when the only English-speaking passenger in the next car became sick and asked me for help. I was able to convey the situation to the provodnika, and she evidently called ahead, for at the next stop a medic stood waiting with a nurse in the middle of the night, and the train had to wait until they had dealt with the passenger. Quite impressive!

Since there was little to see travelling across the vast expanse of Siberia—which is as large as China and India combined, filled with nothing but endless taiga and bushland, and only very occasionally a hamlet with wooden huts and dirt paths—one congregated in the dining car or walked from one car to another. Little groups would form, but to communicate I tended to stay near my Hungarians. Yet the Russians were all friendly with me.

Soon we reached Lake Baikal and thus Irkutsk, where many passengers left and others boarded the express, to make the long trip in two portions. After another day's ride, we crossed the wide Yenisey at Krasnojarsk, and it took nearly three more days to traverse the Siberian Plateau. We also crossed the Ob at Novosibirsk and the Irtysh at Omsk. Shortly after Sverdlovsk (now Yekaterinburg), we passed the Europe-Asia border at Kilometre 1,778 at dusk, and a day and a half later the express rolled into Moscow's Yaroslavl station after 9,300 kilometres and 160 hours of travel, the longest railway journey in the world.

After a night in the prescribed Hotel National, I was delivered to Moscow's domestic airport and had to wait like all the others for my flight to Volgograd (formerly Stalingrad). A while later, being the only foreigner, I was led between two flight attendants to the Aeroflot plane, an Antonov with rear-boarding, to seat number one. Only then were the other sixty passengers allowed to take their places.

During the two-hour flight over the open vastness, I had to think much about the German advance of 1941–42. All that distance, covered by marching! Stalingrad is a sad place for Germans of my generation, because roughly 250,000 men were defeated there in merciless winter fighting. No wonder then that the Russians have erected a giant victory column at Mamayev Hill, the ascent to which is lined with the graves of Soviet generals. The most depressing is the huge memorial dome with a concrete relief showing the exhausted German survivors going into captivity—and only five thousand of the almost one hundred thousand returned home alive.

After landing back at Moscow airport, there was an incident requiring my guardian angel's help. I was not met and picked up by a taxi driver as prescribed by Soviet law. It was an awkward situation, being alone in that totalitarian state! I waited quite a while, then went with passport and ticket in hand to the administration counter to report this—to great consternation! Much running around ensued, until finally an officer showed up with a taxi driver in tow who delivered me properly to the Hotel National, and calm was restored.

I went sightseeing in Moscow for two days before taking the train to Minsk and the border at Brest, where trains were transposed to standard gauge, and on across Poland to Berlin. After visiting my relatives and the family grave (since levelled due to coal mining), I travelled to Amsterdam for the return flight to Montreal and Ottawa, where I arrived on September 18, having logged some 12,600 kilometres on various trains.

Back at home, the old work and study pressures awaited me. I was met with an avalanche of urgent war crime documents needing translation, not to mention my last year of science studies and exams. Only the prospect of it being over soon kept me going. A nice consolation prize was my presentation with the Red Cross certificate for one hundred blood donations and recognition as Humanitarian Citizen of the Year by the City of Gloucester. However, the best gift was the success of the peaceful demonstrations in Leipzig in the fall of 1989, leading to the fall of the Wall and official reunification of Germany in October 1990. Still, one should reflect on the fact that even the now-united country is barely half as large as the German Reich I grew up in as a teen. Sic transit gloria.

The spring and summer of 1989 brought personal highs and lows—much stress and overwork, plus the academic end spurt. I had lots of duties at St. John as well, and in between a quick flight to Victoria to see that things were all right with my rented-out house. In January and May, I finished two more courses each, and thus could observe my sixtieth birthday with sixteen of the seventeen courses in the bag. The last was a difficult math course. After final cramming, I sat for that exam in August, waiting and hoping, until in late September came the relieving news: I had passed it, barely. With that, all requirements for the Bachelor of Science had been met. Thus six years of distance education, involving many different subjects, thirty-three courses, plus some one hundred fifty essays, had come to a successful conclusion. This had been no small feat.

As a reward, I allowed myself another flight to Germany, where we remaining three siblings met once more, as Helmut had come from Australia. In addition, I booked the week from Christmas to New Year's with a small American geological group who, like me, was interested in the Mayan culture and wanted to explore the recently discovered Mirador temple ruins in the extreme north of Guatemala.

That turned out to be quite an adventure with an unpleasant aftereffect. Eight of us met in Guatemala City and flew to Flores, our start and end point. Split into two four-wheel-drive vehicles, our group made the eighty-kilometre trip to Carmelita in four hours. Once there, we obtained the mules ordered beforehand, and rode on them for two days along chicle paths through the jungle, spending the night in mini-tents in a small clearing. The animals had to be left behind while we trekked another two hours to our destination.

Though much of the structure was still covered in tropical vegetation, we enjoyed great views from the top, well into the Yucatán. After investigating the exposed ruins extensively, we started on the return hike and mule ride, which later gave me two nasty surprises. Luckily my guardian angel stepped in, preventing serious damage. We were riding single-file on a narrow path, and close together. On dismounting for a break, my saddle slid sideways, whereupon the mule ahead of me spooked and kicked, striking my quickly raised arm! It swelled and hurt so much that I had to ride all the way back with my arm in a sling—not easy since I had to hold the reins while at the same time bending back obstructing branches.

X-rays taken at the clinic in Flores showed that nothing was broken. However, I also noted that my legs were itching fiercely. I had garrapatas! These are tiny ticks that evidently had clambered by the hundreds from the saddle-cloth and the blanket into my pant legs. It was an ugly and bothersome mess, even more so as back in Canada I had to wear winter socks. Many weeks went by before I could bare my legs to anyone. These disgusting mites annoyed me more than the snakes and scorpions which also occur there—and are common in Honduras, where I lived too.

*The one and only meeting of the remaining four siblings in Detmold, W-Germany
Oct 1986
L-R: Friederun, Ki, Helmut, the author*

*The Trans-Siberian express, the author and his Hungarian compartment mates,
Sep 1988*

Mule ride from Mirador to Carmelita, N-Guatemala, Dec 1989

Chapter Fifteen
My So-Called Retirement (1990–99)

On return, I gave notice of terminating my position with the Translation Bureau, effective July 1990. But I was actually done in mid-March, as I had four months of leave coming. Though there still was much work in the bureau, I needed to concern myself with my upcoming retirement and move to the West Coast—such as preparing my Ottawa townhouse for sale, and the Victoria one to move in. Then came March 16, 1990, my last day at work, with moving send-offs there and later at St. John Ambulance, the Military Engineers, and my church congregation.

Meanwhile, I had prepared another trip to see my Central American foster daughters, who all needed attention. I wanted to meet Vilma (who had succeeded Silvia in Guatemala), Marisol in El Salvador was in her last year of college, and a job had to be found for Azucena in Honduras. The journey to the various SOS Children's Villages went well, and I was cordially received as I had been to each one before. Vilma and Keyla, Azucena's successor, remained my charges for over twelve years each, and Marisol had asked me to attend her graduation in November in lieu of a father. I not only did that, but brought her to Canada to visit me and my daughters.

After attending an MMI project in the Dominican Republic, the time for my move had come. My house was sold, on June 1 the moving van was loaded, and ten days later I flew to my new home in Victoria with my daughter Brigit, who helped me mightily with moving in (my back was troubling me). After almost twenty years in Ontario, as of mid-June 1990 I was home again in British Columbia, where I had arrived nearly forty years earlier as a penniless immigrant. Now I was returning as a retired Canadian public servant!

Another phase in my life had begun: so-called retirement. It was quite a change after forty-two years of working. Suddenly, I wasn't needed or even consulted any more, a colossal waste of experience. It is well-established that pensioners, especially those living alone, succumb early unless they can feel useful again and/or find a new activity. I, on the other hand, had many plans: continued study, more travel, increased social work, care of family ties, and my own social life.

First I had to fix up my house and property to make it homey for the "rest of my life," and I succeeded in that. By the time I unexpectedly moved out fifteen years later, everything was just about as I had wanted it to be! As all homeowners know, one is never really finished. While working, you have money but no time; once retired, you have time but no money! At any rate, I could now arrange my time and tasks as I saw fit, and I set out to increase both my medical mission attendance and my education. Regarding the former, I could now go at other times than July and to places apart from Honduras; regarding the latter, I applied for a Master's program at UVic in Latin American Studies. When that was at long last rejected, for want of a professor in that field, I applied to all kinds of programs at several western universities. Meanwhile, I had become a volunteer director with the Red Cross in Victoria, keeping me busy locally tracing refugees. I had also flown to now-united Germany, attending my sister's seventieth birthday, as well as to Australia to visit my brother and family there.

While waiting to hear back from universities, I participated in a few medical missions. On the one to Salamá in Guatemala in the spring of 1992, I was almost incapacitated by my latent lower back and hip problem, which suddenly flared up again, making for painful walking and sleepless nights. When my roommates complained about my moaning at night, I was taken to the local hospital, where they diagnosed a largely detached ligament. The Lord had the remedy ready in the form of old

Doc Merriman, who years earlier had pioneered a simple procedure to aid reattachment and was now anxious to prove it. It involved dextrose injections directly onto the bone/ligament site, and I got 185 of them after mild sedation. The treatment was, indeed, successful. Apart from the predicted short relapse three months later, the problem has over time practically disappeared.

Meanwhile, the various university replies came in, mostly negative because of quotas or my age, notably from the Medical School in Calgary and University of Waterloo's School of Optometry, despite my two good undergraduate degrees there. As I was mulling things over, the Lord again pointed the way: just then, UVic, together with four other western universities, had put together the so-called CACE program, a new diploma for adult-education teachers. I applied right away and was accepted for the next trimester—a kind of consolation prize for the other rejections—and was suddenly very busy. This would be the beginning of six more increasingly intensive years of studies, which produced a string of four graduations. That came about because I later entered Pacific Western's distance program for a Master's, and ultimately for a doctorate, while concurrently attending the CACE and later Applied Linguistics courses at UVic, in person. Needless to say, in those years I could manage only one medical mission per year, but that grew to four or five after finishing my doctorate in late 1997.

There were some personal events worth mentioning in those years. Owing to my academic efforts, I retired from St. John Ambulance duties at age sixty-five. Before that, I had made the acquaintance of a rather fetching newcomer named Maxine, with whom I went on St. John and Red Cross duties together and later studied with side-by-side. She stayed at my house for a while, but soon left to join the Navy. My own commitment to the SRR (Supplementary Ready Reserve) also ended on my sixty-fifth birthday. I was finally fully civilian again!

With the UVic diploma and the PWU Master's degree in the bag, in 1996 I undertook another grand-slam trip to Central America, visiting all my four foster daughters in Guatemala, El Salvador, Nicaragua, and Honduras. All were doing well, as were my own daughters in Ottawa, one finishing her high school leaving certificate, the other teaching languages.

During my CACE studies, I had come into contact with a fellow student named Dorothy in Prince George, whom I encountered every time teleconferences were held to accommodate out-of-town students. We stayed in touch and helped each other with the assignments. Though rather restricted by her juvenile diabetes, she returned my visit just in time for the December 1996 "Blizzard of the Century" here in Victoria, with three feet of snow. When she lost her job and lease, I invited her to move into my recently finished granny flat, initially for a year to finish her CACE program. That stretched into three years—during which she helped me complete my dissertation—that is, until she returned to her native Edmonton, when the University of Alberta offered a new kind of transplant treatment for patients like her. We have remained good friends, and the Lord would soon steer me toward someone else.

In November 1997, I received my PhD at Pacific Western University in Los Angeles, at the ripe old age of sixty-eight. With God's help and my own tenacity, I had passed through the entire academic range in fifteen years and earned six credentials in different fields, mainly Adult Education and Linguistics.

Now I was free to pursue travel and other interests. I went on a VDK tour to Normandy (VDK standing for Volksbund Deutsche Kriegsgräberfürsorge, or in English, the German War Graves Commission). I had been to Stalingrad, and would soon see Narvik, Monte Cassino, and Budapest. All these places are deep in my memory, as they were much in the news when I was a teen—and practically all families in Germany were affected by one or more of these battles. The scale of those war events never ceases to amaze me, with literally millions of combatants fighting for years. And what did this enormous conflagration accomplish or settle? Was this struggle and its outcome God's will, and if so, why did so many innocent people have to die? Why they, and not me? We won't know the answers until we are in the next world.

Next, I went on more missions, and on one—to El Carmen in Ecuador in November 1998—I again felt my guardian angel hard at work. It was Friday afternoon and our team had finished its work. We were on the way back to Quito for the last night before flying home. We were riding in a big bus, in cold weather and sleet some ten thousand feet up, on a winding road about thirty kilometres from the capital, when the driver decided to overtake a slow-moving tractor-trailer combination on a short straight stretch. He misjudged the time it would take and thus was not yet past it when approaching the next bend—out of which came a passenger car at fairly high speed! With insufficient room to squeeze through, the car struck the left front of the bus, glancing off it and careening shrilly along its side—right where I sat! With only an inch of metal between us, I could see the shock on the car driver's face and then hear the crash of the car. Our bus stopped, and its driver disappeared into the night! Myself and the two Canadian nurses on board jumped out and to the car, which lay on its side. It was too late for the driver, but his passenger lived, bleeding from a scalp wound and suffering from shock. We fixed him up as well as we could and stayed with him until the police came almost an hour later. They bundled him on their pick-up and drove him to the hospital. We visited him the next morning, and he made it. It took a while to get a replacement driver, so we got to Quito late and somewhat shaken from the close call.

The following year, 1999, would be much nicer. Not only could I go with my brother-in-law Armin and his camper to Narvik, Norway in June, and also with my daughters to see my brother in Australia in September for a belated seventieth birthday celebration, but in between I attended an Eye Project in Olanchito, Honduras. The trip was noteworthy for two reasons. First, the country was only beginning to emerge from the devastation caused by Hurricane Mitch the year before, which had resulted in many thousands dead or missing and destroyed seventy percent of its infrastructure. Second, I met Elia, a local volunteer helping our team.

Little did I know it then, but the Lord was already at work bringing us together, unlikely as it may sound: a seventy-year-old white professional and a mestizo woman half his age? Yet Elia told me later that even then she knew we would marry one day. Amazingly, two years later, we did! Back then, she worked as a nurse's aide in the local old folks' home in Olanchito, her hometown and where I also lived half of each year. She was bringing her charges to our clinic and took them home again after they had been examined or had surgery. She had to take the cataract patients to me for working up, thus I saw her on several occasions in those two weeks, a few minutes each time. She certainly was nice to look at, with dark hair and bronze skin. She also had a little tummy, but that didn't register with me; only the somewhat downcast expression didn't seem to fit. When I asked her about it towards the end of our mission, the truth came out: she was pregnant and without support! Since that is unfortunately a common occurrence there, I asked our director whether this case merited assistance; she referred me to the lady in charge of the old folks' home, who assured me that Elia was a very good woman.

When we were about to leave, our female interpreter found under her door a note addressed to the "Canadian sisters in Christ," asking urgently for help. She gave me the note and said, "Do with it whatever you want," and we all flew home.

Although I had received similar requests in the past and replied to them without ever getting a reaction, I couldn't stop thinking about this one. Therefore I translated Elia's scribbled note and sent copies to said Canadian sisters, asking them for contributions. Since only two materialized, I added a fair bit and mailed the cheque to the address given in Olanchito. With that, I considered the matter closed. However, the Lord had other plans.

Arriving at my "retirement home" in Victoria, BC Jun 1990

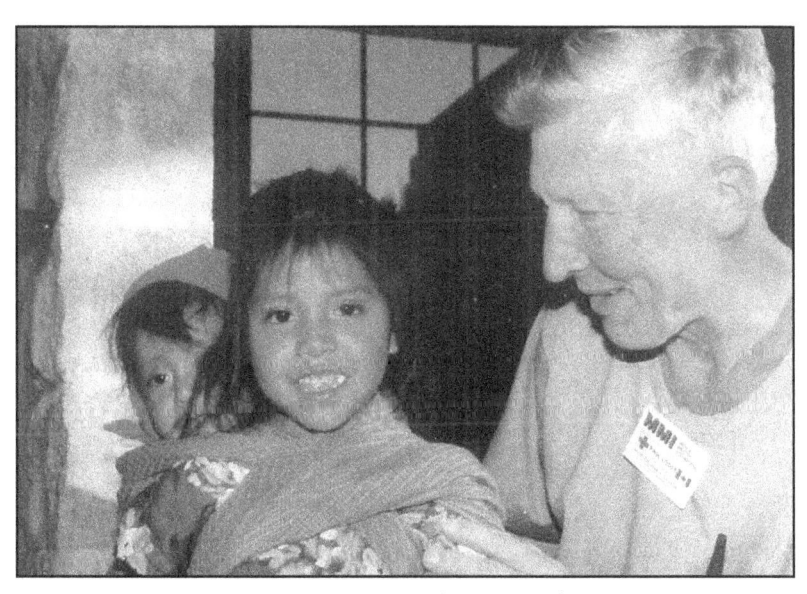

Medical Mission to Comitancillo, Guatemala Jan 1999

At the Arctic Circle nr Mo-i-Rana, northern Norway, Jun 1999

With my daughters and my brother in Sydney, Australia, Sep 1999

Chapter Sixteen
Living in Two Cultures (2000–2019)

The Millennium Year was an eventful one for me. Elia surprised me positively by writing me a thank-you note, and then when her son was born, by asking my consent to name him Paul, after me. The ensuing correspondence (with air mail letters taking at least a month round-trip) got more and more personal, so I decided to look her up the following year in conjunction with the next Eye Project in La Esperanza, Honduras, in July 2000.

After a long bus ride to Olanchito, the taxi driver finally located her uncle and aunt's place (there are few street signs or house numbers) where Elia had been living for years. I was received with slight astonishment but very kindly, and several other relatives also came. I had the feeling of being examined in a fashion—evidently, such a visit is interpreted as looking for a bride! Elia herself did not say much—she is basically a quiet person—but occupied herself with little Paul, whom I could now look at more closely. They put me up for the night, and the next morning I had to return all the way to San Pedro. From there I flew to San Salvador and visited the new SOS Village of Izalco to meet my foster son José. I also saw Marisol and her sister Xiomara once more, my last visit—all are grown up and independent now.

Apart from this intriguing development with Elia, that year also saw me flying to Europe again, mainly because my brother and his wife had come from Australia, and also because I wanted to see the new VDK

Peace Park in Budaörs, Hungary. The soldiers buried there died near the end of the war and many of them had been very young, only a year or two older than I was at the time.

I rode the train to my sister's place in Detmold for, as it has turned out, the last meeting of the surviving three siblings (then seventy-nine, seventy-three, and seventy-one years old). After somewhat sad goodbyes from my sister and her husband (who have since died), Helmut, Sigi, and I went to our brother-in-law Armin's place near Colditz, including a visit to Ki's grave, and lastly to Leipzig. We used the opportunity for a streetcar ride to Markkleeberg and even to the parental house, where I had arrived into the world and grown up long ago. After another day in Leipzig this nostalgic trip came to an end, as the Australians had a busy schedule elsewhere and I had to return via Berlin to Canada.

As a pensioner living alone, it is easy to start brooding, especially in the damp and chilly winters here on the West Coast, with so many dull days. That my remaining brother and sister, and now also my wife, lived in different continents, and even my daughters are far away, is tough. In addition, there are now more and more deaths in my circle of relatives and friends, as well as among classmates and military buddies. Even my days as a blood donor came to an end on reaching the age limit; after fifty years, that part of my life would be missed, though I remained a Red Cross helper for some time yet. I liked the feeling that came from being able to help directly; that's also why the medical missions of MMI Canada have been so important to me. Like in the Red Cross, there one is among altruistic people who bring medical and spiritual aid to the needy in the name of Jesus. I seem to get along with these simple fellow men quite well, and apparently not only because I make an effort to understand their language and culture. Therefore, I feel called upon even at my age to apply my acquired knowledge of language, human nature, and practical experience to the benefit of needy people, believing I can still contribute something of value as an instrument of our Lord.

I was happy to make it onto a small team going to Caagazú in Paraguay, where we worked with the local Mennonite community among mainly Guarani Indian patients. The trilingual work, and especially the farewell dinner under the Southern Cross, were unforgettable, as was the visit to the grand Iguazú Falls.

The new millennium began with hope, built up to a happy climax, and then deteriorated into personal hardship and an international crisis. My correspondence with Elia was now warm, for my visit there had been taken as proof of great interest, which was reciprocated by her. She knew by now that I was divorced and lived alone. True, I had taken a shine to Elia, but given the big difference in age and culture, I hadn't thought at first that she could be—or would even want to be—considered a romantic prospect. But when she wrote me, saying that a "nice man like you deserves a good woman," I thought to myself, *Maybe so, but where do I find one?* Unless of course she meant herself, which I still thought unlikely in view of her unassuming nature. I therefore replied with something like "It would be nice," and listed some reasons why we wouldn't be a compatible couple. She in turn invalidated each one by saying: "In case of genuine love, none of those matter!"

This way of looking at it made the whole situation appear in a different light, and I began to ask myself, "Why not?" I was still in pretty good shape, fairly familiar with the language and culture there (or so I thought), and after years alone quite receptive to female company. Also, Elia had a baby boy, who would soon need a father and who could take the place of my missing grandchildren, since my daughters had chosen to remain childless. Though I had more in common with my friend Dorothy than with Elia, the balance tipped in favour of the latter, now that Dorothy had been accepted into the transplant program in Edmonton and was thus taken care of.

After meeting with Elia and little Paul in the team hotel at the end of another mission to Honduras in March, and after talking things over, many reservations were removed. On the other hand, more than one attractive prospect had slipped away because I had hesitated too long, so I thought, *Nothing ventured, nothing gained.* I proposed to Elia by mail, having received my daughters' approval. Several weeks later, Elia's reply came—not a yes or no, but rather "when and where?"

Without a doubt, this would be a daring enterprise. We had known each other only a few days, lived several thousand kilometres apart in different countries, and differed in age by over thirty years. She also had a toddler and no home. All that was apart from the obvious differences in language, culture, and education. It would be the second time for both of us, and we were quite determined to learn from previous mistakes and make this improbable marriage work. Thanks to God and our resolve, we enjoyed almost twenty years of married life.

We now needed to find a home. The Spanish term for getting married is "casarse," from the word "casa," meaning house. Translated literally, it means "putting yourself into a house." Well, that was a long and costly process. It took over a year and was ultimately resolved by having to buy a lot and build one (where one must not apply first-world standards). To afford to build this new home, I sold my house in Victoria and instead found an apartment to live while there.

Despite this, technically we were not even married; that was to happen in connection with the next Eye Clinic in Yoro. But who could know beforehand that it would take three runs at it to succeed?

The wedding was scheduled for July 27 in El Progreso, to where our team would be returning. I had to take the Castros, our MMI directors, into my confidence to get them to hold the excursion bus that Friday morning until Elia and I had come back from the registry office. Elia had already joined us the previous evening for the traditional final dinner, at which time Señora Castro couldn't resist announcing our impending marriage, to tumultuous applause.

On this Friday (the registry office there marries people only on Fridays), we were rejected because we had not given two weeks' notice. But we couldn't stay until the next Friday, and our witnesses would not have been available then. So we had to return, Elia to Olanchito, I to Victoria, only for me to fly back alone to El Progreso in August. I had registered us at the same hotel by air mail and faxed Elia to come in time for the ceremony on August 24. I had also had the wedding announcements printed for that date. But when I arrived, there was nobody at the airport, nor did anybody greet me at the hotel. Worst of all, there was no Elia—and weddings without a bride are no fun! Evidently my letter had not yet arrived. It came three days later! Elia had gotten the fax, but she'd forgotten the date. Luckily my angel helped by establishing telephone contact via her aunt that night.

Elia had to hop on the 3:00 a.m. bus to make it in time for our 10:00 slot. But oh horror, when it was finally our turn, the city clerk told us that for me, as a foreigner, permission from my government was needed! This meant travelling to the Canadian embassy in the capital, which of course was not possible until Monday, automatically postponing the wedding to the following Friday. The days in between then became our honeymoon week, for neither of us could stay longer afterwards, and Elia missed her son very much already. The civil wedding did take place on Friday, August 31, 2001. We each said "Sí," signed the register, and exchanged rings. The four witnesses (two from MMI, and two from the city) beamed, the mayor handed us the certificate, and then we were officially husband and wife!

Yet, as so often happens in life, this high was soon followed by a low. Actually, two hard blows. On September 11 occurred the terrorist attack on the World Trade Center in New York—the first enemy action on American soil since Pearl Harbour sixty years earlier. That attack completely surprised the United States and shook it to the core. In the following hysteria, it seemed advisable to postpone Elia's first visit to Canada; it would take place next summer instead.

The other blow concerned me directly. At my routine examination that fall, an elevated PSA value—a potential cancer indicator—was found and a biopsy scheduled. Meanwhile, I could attend another Eye Mission in Mexico, and then take my daughters to the Pier 21 Historic Site in Halifax, where I had stepped ashore fifty years earlier. Afterwards, I had to undergo the biopsy, and soon I was confronted with the bad news: "You have cancer!"

That churns you up pretty badly and forces you to grapple with the unpleasant truth and wrestle with the old "why me?" question. I passed through the well-known stages of grief to more or less resigned acceptance. This process took several months, but also confirmed what St. Paul states in Romans 5:3–5—namely, that our tribulations bring about perseverance, and perseverance character, and character hope—and hope does not disappoint.

For many years, the Lord has let me carry on without requiring so-called treatment (actually, the destruction of the gland). However, with much higher PSA levels now, that grace period has come to an end.

I had to inform Elia of this awkward fact, and I did so early in December. I explained the situation and the likely consequences to her, then offered to release her from our young marriage under the circumstances. The fact that she immediately rejected that idea has brought her much appreciation with me and my family. Just the same, it was and is difficult to grin and bear it, especially being practically alone half the year (I must be in Canada six months a year to be covered by my federal health insurance). One ponders the meaning of life, and suddenly the efforts one has made to gain honours or position appear meaningless, or in the words of a hymn, "And the things of earth grow strangely dim in the light of His glory and peace."

Eventually, I had to pull myself together again and carry on. God still had tasks for me to perform, such as caring for the family and doing charity work—proven antidotes for the dangers of falling victim to self-pity and lethargy. These are also good reasons for continuing to participate in as many medical missions as are financially and physically possible.

Over the past few years, the Lord has allowed me to go on quite a few, and on some with my wife. On one such occasion, after finishing a mission in West Honduras in November 2002, my guardian angel had to swing into action again. At the recreational swim afterwards at the beach of Tela, I almost drowned. Despite fairly big waves, I had entered the water once more, alone—and ended up in an undercurrent, from which I got out only with difficulty. Though in fairly shallow water, the waves knocked me down into the swirling sand every time, barely allowing me to come up for air. It was quite scary! Yet I considered myself a good swimmer and even had earned the basic lifesaver certificate as a young man. All the while, Elia and a few others were sitting in an open beach house and saw me flailing my arms; she thought it was for joy! She couldn't have helped, as she only dog-paddles. The Lord's angel did the work, guiding me out of harm's way.

Though I had been briefly to Holland and Belgium on the occasion of the Centenary of the Canadian Military Engineers in 2003 and taken part in the thirty-three-kilometre Knokke-Heist Liberation March, I flew to Germany a year later. That was to participate in another VDK trip to Normandy, for the sixtieth anniversary of the invasion. I also was going to celebrate my sister's golden wedding anniversary and attend the sixtieth anniversary of my own confirmation in the historic Thomas church in Leipzig. It was moving to stand among those elderly people who had lived in the faith all their lives. While there, I also did a sentimental walk around the sites and streets of my childhood and youth, with many memories surging up. I had a lot to digest and reflect on during the flight back to Canada.

Elia accompanied me on two medical missions to Honduras, in November 2004, my fiftieth overall, and in February 2005, my thirtieth in Honduras. She came to the latter, because it took place for the first time in Olancho, her home province; she could thus visit her birthplace and her parents (as opposed to her uncle and aunt in Olanchito, who had raised her as a teen). It is an awkward journey, in old school busses, into this remote area and, owing to bandits, rather risky. Guardian angels needed! An armed policeman rides on every bus, and we even saw two Pepsi trucks with guards riding shotgun—just like in the Wild West. The whole region feels like that, with the occasional man on horseback riding by, and more than one passenger sporting a pistol on his belt. In the meantime, the drug gangs in Mexico and Colombia have faced increasingly tough times, so they have moved to the poorly policed Central America, with devastating effect. It has become unsafe, and in 2012 Honduras had the depressing distinction of being the world's most violent country (according to *The Economist* magazine), with now ninety murders per one hundred thousand people—some thirty times the Canadian rate!

Back in 2004, my asthmatic neighbour Jane was found dead one day and nobody noticed, for she was a quiet person. The nice old neighbour in the apartment on the other side, who had been a WWII medic and worked as a hospital orderly all his life, also died. Moreover, by now Brigit suffered from clinical depression, and Karen from burnout. All these events made me pensive, especially because I lived alone. Therefore, travelling to Latin America, where life generally is simpler and time pressures and worries about the future take a backseat, can be salutary. It also makes me appreciate my wife's calm nature.

Though I was, of course, concerned about my daughters' well-being, I had to do something about my wife's visa problems, as she wanted to not only join me on the Eye Clinic in Mexico that summer, but also to visit Canada. We finally wanted to have a church wedding, and that was to take place in Victoria.

Since the 9/11 terrorist attack, it has become harder for Central Americans to obtain North American visas. Mexico fears becoming a stepping-stone for illegal entry into the United States, and the United States and Canada worry that such visitors will then disappear rather than return. The fact that Elia was my lawful wife and that we left our son at home in Honduras wasn't enough then. It helped, therefore, to have the Canadian visa in your passport first, so the Mexican one won't be a problem. That method worked in the end, but only after we had travelled to the Canadian embassy in Guatemala City and Elia was interviewed as to why she didn't want to stay in Canada, since I am Canadian. She soon got both the Canadian and Mexican visas, so we could proceed.

The Eye Project in Queretaro went very well. We saw some six thousand people and performed over three hundred surgeries, handing out four thousand pairs of eyeglasses—and this time Elia and I could work side by side. As several patients noticed that we were a couple, word got around and gave us an edge with the people. Afterwards, I escorted Elia back to Honduras where we had to separate, as she could not leave her son any longer, and as I had a lot to catch up with and prepare in Canada.

My pastor in Victoria had already done the groundwork for the wedding. The only item missing was someone other than me to read the Spanish text. Here again, the Lord helped wondrously. When a granddaughter of my deceased godmother Ida called me out of the blue (her husband had just been transferred to Victoria), it turned out that she was a Spanish teacher. Problem solved! The bilingual ceremony was to take place on Sunday, August 28, 2005 (practically our fourth wedding anniversary).

I felt obliged to pick Elia up in Honduras and escort her here. Despite a rather higher PSA level, I flew to Honduras, spent a week with my family there, and then returned with Elia to Canada via Toronto and Ottawa. We had three days with my daughters, where at one dinner some fun was made about me and "my three women," as all were about the same age, even though they looked and spoke rather differently. We were also invited to the national offices of both SOS Children's Villages Canada and CARE-Canada (I am well-known at both organizations). I appreciated the opportunity to let Elia see their work, particularly in Honduras.

On arrival in Victoria, we were met by church friends and enjoyed a beautiful week in this garden city on the Pacific. The high point, of course, was the Sunday service on August 28, followed by the English/Spanish marriage ceremony, which went off nicely and in a dignified manner. It was celebrated warmly with a congregational reception afterwards. Thus we now have a Honduran civil marriage certificate, as of August 2001, and a Canadian church wedding certificate, as of August 2005. We are doubly secure!

The following weekend, we took the four flights to Honduras together and then rode the bus all the way to Olanchito—my routine every other month now for years—to be there for Elia's birthday, and also to speak with the new missionary pastor from Nicaragua, with the result that devotions were held on our porch. The rainy season starts thereabouts by late summer. Just before my departure, the roof began to leak, a common annoyance. One puts a bucket underneath and carries on as per normal.

On my return to Canada, I had to note that there was little improvement regarding my daughters' state of health. Fortunately, they are fine now. My PSA level had even come down a bit, so the oncologist let me go on for another year; I live from one test to another and can only hope and pray. Lord, Your will be done.

Even in the last few years, I have felt the Lord's helping hand, apart from His protection on my near-constant travel to and from Central and South America. Several examples make the point.

One day in Olanchito in October 2006, I was working as usual on our small piece of land, which boasts some trees. I noticed a dead branch on one and proceeded to cut it, having borrowed a makeshift ladder. While looking up and sawing the branch, the third leg attached to the A-frame gave way, and I crashed to the ground—how exactly, I do not remember. Little Paul saw it happen from a distance and called his mother; the two helped me up and insisted on taking me to the Christian hospital, thanks to a neighbour's car. There they took X-rays, which showed one rib broken and another one cracked, otherwise no real damage apart from pain. My guardian angel had saved me from worse, and I recovered nicely over the following weeks.

In Honduras, 2009 is remembered as the year of the most recent "golpe de estado" (coup d'état). There have been almost 150 in its barely two-hundred-year history. I was there that June, and it was distressing to watch events unfold, with political repercussions persisting to this day.

More scary on a personal level was another potentially grave incident in the fall of the same year. Elia and I had just returned from an exciting one-week tour of the Holy Land—an unforgettable experience in itself, walking at times on sites that He walked on two thousand years before—and after a short stay in Olanchito, I had to return to Canada. As usual, we travelled together by bus to El Progreso, stayed there overnight, and then took the taxi for the half-hour ride to the airport of San Pedro Sula. I was sitting in the front seat next to the driver, and Elia with our bags on the rear bench.

With hardly any traffic at 5:30 in the morning, we were travelling at a good clip. After a while, I thought I could feel a front-wheel shimmy and mentioned that to the driver, who basically said not to worry. Not even two minutes later, there was a whooshing sound, followed by loud screeching and dancing sparks. The left front wheel had broken loose from the drum (only two studs had been holding it, we found) and rolled a long way off to the side. At the same time, the driver hung on grimly to the steering wheel, coaxing his now three-wheeled taxi to a controlled stop along the edge of the highway. I don't know how many angels it took to steer the vehicle safely to a halt; it was amazing.

Elia didn't say a word. She wasn't aware of the seriousness of what had happened until later. It was something to tell when we enjoyed a most unusual family meet the following year: my brother and his wife came from Australia, I had managed to bring Elia up from Honduras, and my daughters flew in from Ontario for that rare occasion which will certainly not occur again.

The past several years have again yielded remarkable events showcasing God's power and love, all in conjunction with medical missions in Latin America. In June 2011, I took part in the first amphibious mission to isolated villages on the Peruvian side of the Amazon River. Our small team (ten North Americans and five locals) met in Leticia at the southernmost tip of Colombia, then went upstream, working at several hamlets over the next two weeks.

These places consist of a few houses on stilts and sometimes a tiny church, practically devoid of so-called facilities, so you went to the bathroom outside at night. On such an occasion on the second last day, I was bitten in my right heel, likely by a snake. In any case, the incisions festered and required antibiotics. A few days later, after returning to Honduras, I began to feel quite weak and feverish, to the point of shaking. Elia had me taken to the lab, and soon the tests showed that I had contracted malaria! Fortunately, the doctors were familiar with that, and the one in the private clinic nearby—another angel—knew exactly what to prescribe and in what combination and sequence for this relatively mild type. He didn't even charge me, being a colleague. I just had to pay for the medicines. Lab tests back in Canada a month later showed I was free of parasites. Thank God!

On our next Eye Project in Sucre, Bolivia in March 2012, I became involved in an amazing sequence of small events that combined, by the grace of God, to save the eyesight of a nineteen-year-old student named Ricardo. He came to our consulting station because of his poor vision. Our ophthalmologist found a detached retina in one eye and asked me to explain that to the patient, adding that all we could do was refer him to the specialist in Santa Cruz. This required an appointment, travelling there, and finding room and board and post-op care—a tall order.

Just then, another ophthalmologist came back from the hospital and checked the patient once more. He discovered a tear in the other retina, making for a dire prognosis: the young man could go blind within weeks! I called in our medical director, who knew the specialist personally; he soon came, examined the patient himself, and agreed to contact the specialist. With the help of our assistant Mariela, we actually got the specialist on the line. Our director pleaded his case, and the specialist promised to fit the patient in the next morning! We then succeeded in locating the patient's sister and talked her into accompanying him, as he would need her to take care of him after bilateral eye surgery. Then there was the matter of transportation to Santa Cruz, three hundred kilometres distant. Our Dr. Hoines and his wife generously paid the airfare for the two. Mariela was able to secure the tickets right at closing time!

The cost for the surgery and laser treatment was quoted at several thousand dollars. However, our medical directors managed to negotiate that down to $2,500—nice, but still a large sum. Fortunately, two team members had a few hundred dollars in church-raised funds available, and all the rest was subscribed in an impromptu reverse auction organized by the director that night! Early the next morning, our assistant drove Ricardo and sister to the airport and saw them off to Santa Cruz. That same afternoon, we received calls that they had arrived at the hospital and that the surgeries had been performed successfully.

After a few days, the pair returned to Sucre, full of praise for the whole operation. Ricardo even showed up at the airport when we left, hugging each of us who had been involved in his road to treatment and healing. It was quite emotional. We also learned that Ricardo had been brought up as a Christian, but had drifted away as a youngster. After seeing Christian love in action, he has returned to the fold—and his vision in both eyes is quite good again, praise the Lord!

A few months later, in July 2012, I was in a fix trying to join the MMI Eye Project in Ayacucho, Peru, coming from my "second home" in Olanchito, Honduras. The flight from San Pedro Sula to San Salvador, which originated in New York, couldn't leave from there for hours because of windstorms in the area—causing me to miss all connections to Lima and beyond. Though the airline advised our Peruvian director, there was nobody at the airport in Lima when I arrived there on the agreed-upon flight one day late. I thus had no onward information or overnight arrangement, and without a cell phone I had no way of communicating with our director.

I had been standing there uneasily for nearly an hour, wondering what to do next, when my guardian angel made me look over the crowd of people, already expecting passengers on another late flight. Among them I noticed a cluster of three Peruvian women, one of whom was holding a German flag. That was most unusual! I walked over to talk to them, and it turned out that the flag holder was married to a German who was supposed to arrive on the next flight. We chatted for a while, even in German, and on learning of my predicament the couple let me use their cell phone to call my director. Communication was established. Problem solved! God works in truly wonderful ways!

Even now while I am translating this book (2014/2015), two events have occurred in Honduras which have shown divine intervention and merciful action by the guardian angel, preventing greater damage.

On our piece of land stands a large old tree which provides shadow, but now also impairs the growth of a young mango tree in front of it. Therefore a big branch was to be removed, and I wanted to do that on my visit in February, 2014. To that end, I had to climb up some three meters above the top of the ladder, hold on to the trunk with one hand, and saw that branch off with the other hand. All went well, except when the branch was breaking off, the one above it, having lost some support, also crashed down with a loud noise—and my hand in between! I was able to pull it almost completely out in time but for my little finger, which caught the full force and was thus squashed, causing considerable bleeding. The trick now was to get down as quickly as possible without fainting—not easy with only one hand, much pain and loss of blood. With the help of my guardian angel I managed to descend all right and bandage the hand provisionally. When Elia returned from shopping, we went to the emergency clinic where they gave me a tetanus shot and antibiotics, and the doctor on duty sewed my finger together again. A week later the stitches were removed and the finger was healed satisfactorily, albeit somewhat curved.

That same summer, we had applied for a visitor's visa for Elia and sent all the forms and her passport as prescribed by courier to the new VAC (Visa Application Centre) in the capital, Tegucigalpa. The application went "missing" for three months! Thank heavens, our angel had it discovered again (in the courier's depot); however, we still had to make the arduous trip to the VAC in person, because now the forms have to be completed by computer.

During my visit in November we received a telephone call for Elia: "Your passport is here, but you must come here yourself, as we do not mail anything out anymore." That was four days before my departure back to Canada, and it meant travelling the $5^1/_2$ hours to El Progreso again, and another $4^1/_2$ hours to Tegucigalpa, plus hotel nights and taxis. Yet we still did not know whether the visa requested had been granted or not, as only the passport holder is authorized to open the package—thus great tension!

Meanwhile, it had been raining heavily for days, and when we went to the bus terminal at 3 a.m., there weren't any busses. The road had washed out, and nothing could go anywhere. There are hardly any official announcements or notices on such occasions, but the night watchman suggested, "Come back tomorrow." The next day a bus did leave, but it only went about one-third of the distance, to the place near Planes where an avalanche of gravel and mud had torn away almost fifty meters of roadbed. Everybody had to get off. Elia and I, and most of the other passengers, scrambled or slid down a steep slippery path, through a calf-high roaring creek, and then back up the other side. Just as we were climbing up the opposite embankment, Elia, who was behind me, screamed, "*corre, corre!*" ("run, run!"). More mud and gravel was cascading down. My guardian angel gave me the presence of mind and the strength to grab Elia's arm and together we escaped from the danger zone by leaps and bounds. We made it! We were both rather dirty when we arrived at the other side of the road, where another bus stood, waiting to take us the rest of the way. We reached El Progreso that evening and the capital the next day. There, Elia received her passport, complete with Canadian visa. What a relief!

What takes a long time will turn out well—or, all's well that ends well. Even so, I had to fly back to Canada alone, as it was too late to arrange flights for Elia and make the other preparations. We had to postpone her visit until the spring, which was just as well, for then Elia could be with me around Easter during my eye surgery. This was very convenient.

By then I was spending almost as much time in Honduras as in Canada—with the occasional interruption of another medical mission—and had become well accustomed to the Honduran way of life. Elia and I had grown really close and worked well together and apart: "When you're here, you're the boss; when you're away, I am" she would say (in Spanish). We had no quarrels; differences of opinion were resolved and/or forgiven before going to bed. She kept house nicely and did the shopping, while I did the yard work and repairs. I had dug up old trees and planted cocos palms, banana and orange trees, and later mango. The place was tidy, and we were on good terms with all the neighbours. Paul did alright at school (unfortunately, he remained the only child), and life went on nicely. The Lord was good to us, even if it meant a lot of travelling for me to look after both places. Money was thus tight, but my credit was good, so we managed. In September 2015 Elia and I went on our last Medical Mission together, to Ica in Peru, and enjoyed working that small team there.

Then (2016) came some unpleasant surprised, both in Honduras and elsewhere. A couple of years earlier I had been introduced to a group called "Friends of Oratorio" that pushed for the premiere of KZ—survivor Peter Gary's work, A 20th Century Passion, in Jerusalem. I had translated the libretto, and was to attend in April. However, the performance was postponed, yet I had already booked some of my flights. Just then my eldest sister died in Germany. Therefore I flew to her funeral from Honduras and returned to Olanchito afterwards. I picked up Elia—we had succeeded in getting her visa—and travelled jointly to Victoria, where I underwent cataract surgery. Two weeks later we returned to Honduras, and I left in July alone for Ottawa to see my daughters and then home to Victoria—all told, the equivalent of around the world again.

That Fall I spent a month in Honduras to observe our 15th wedding anniversary and Elia's birthday in good spirits. However, towards the end Elia became uneasy about something in her breast. We agreed to have it checked out—meaning a trip to La Ceiba, the nearest reliable clinic two hours away—and I left from there. At my next visit, in

November—I had been in Israel and attended the Oratorio's premiere there, plus events in Germany in October—the bad news hit: the biopsy had shown breast cancer! Now Elia had to struggle with that blow, and it hit her hard. Thanks to her firm faith, she passed through the difficult stages to eventual acceptance—so hard for a woman of not even fifty! It was a tough time for both of us, with me feeling so helpless, except for being with her as much as possible. We all agreed on the best treatment option: the recent American-style (and priced) Cancer Clinic outside the Hospital in San Pedro Sula—six hours by bus, plus overnight stay, city bus and taxis each time for each chemo, five times in November and December alone. After several chemos the next Spring (2017), which seemed to help, surgery was urged upon poor Elia; it took place in May, and she was now considered "cured". We all prayed a lot asking for God's mercy, and for months all appeared well, at least with the help of radiation sessions in San Pedro Sula.

In September I flew to Australia to be with my brother on his 90th birthday, which we celebrated with a last joint trip into the Interior to see the famous Uluru (ex Ayer's) Rock; then said good-bye.

Yet to our horror, during my visits the following Summer and Fall (2018), we could see and feel metastasis had occurred at the neck, then shoulder and arm. Despite frantic treatment with new chemo pills and more radiation, there was no stopping. By October, all that could be done was medicating the increasing pain…

Elia's mother and two surviving sons (she had lost two already) had come in September for moral support and were still there when I arrived in late November. Son Paul turned 19 then; he had graduated the year before and applied to the Military Academy, but failed to make the cut. All the family were now very concerned about Elia's chances, and I left quite worried for Victoria and Ottawa to be with my daughters in mid-December. Christmas came and went, and more disturbing news, until I got a call in early January that Elia had only "a week or two left" to live…

Long before I had booked for the customary Eye-Mission in Bolivia in February 2019; I managed to move my departure by way of Honduras forward to January 18th—but the dreaded call of Elia's death came two days earlier: The Lord had ended her pain on 15 January 2019.

When I arrived on the 18th, the house was chock full with family and friends, mourners coming and going. The funeral had already taken place—by Honduran law, it must be within 24 hours—and there was now little I could do. After a full week, everybody left—and I was literally and emotionally alone. So I attended to legal and financial matters, bequeathing the house and property to son Paul and most of the contents to his uncle and godfather Ramón, now that I would lose my resident status in Olanchito. Then I left Honduras to join the MMI-team to Yapatani, Bolivia, which helped me by doing that altruistic work among the poor.

Thanks to Dr. Snow, with whom I had worked before, I could join a CCSHH (Honduran Christian Charity) eye team to Olanchito in May 2019 and work there in the local hospital (where Elia had done her med/tech practicum years ago), sometimes even with Paul. On the weekend after the team had left, I could thus briefly visit the family and say goodbye to them and Honduras, thinking it to be the last time.

*The last meeting of us the three remaining siblings in Detmold, Germany, Sept 2000
L-R: the author, Helmut, Friederun*

Our house in Olanchito, Honduras 2003

The family in Olanchito, Nov 2008
L-R: Elia, son Paul, the author

Unique family reunion in Victoria, BC in July 2010
*L-R: Helmut and Sigi (AUS), Karen, Brigit, and Mark (ON), Elia (HON)
and the author (BC&HON)*

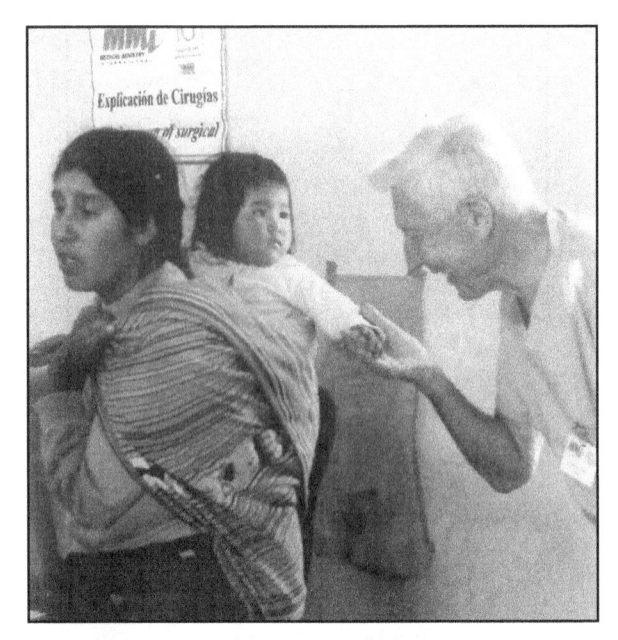

At the MMI Project Ayacucho, S Peru, Jul 2012

The Loofs Family (Elia, Paul, and Pablo) in Olanchito, Honduras, Nov. 2013

Chapter Seventeen
Sunset (2020 and beyond)

Early in January 2020 God provided another opportunity. Dr. Snow had mentioned in his Christmas card that he and his colleague Dr. Turley would go on another CCSHH Mission to Honduras in January. Then he notified me that the clinic site have been changed to Olanchito, from 23-31 January 2020. This piqued my interest: I could then combine it with a weekend to see son Paul and Elia's grave with the new plaque. After a flurry of e-mails (thanks to my in-house friend Nigel), I was accepted again to the same team as last May.

So off I went to San Pedro Sula, where we all met and drove in CCSHH's new station wagon to Olanchito for a week of hard and often late work, completing some 130 cataract surgeries in the local hospital. On that last Friday the 31st, after a reception by the mayor, the team said good-bye and left on the long ride back to El Progreso, whereas I was left alone until finally picked up from the hotel. Thus I spent the remainder of Friday and all day Saturday at the house of Elia's cousin Maria Teresa—exactly one year after the agreement giving our property to son Paul (with option to buy for his uncle Ramón) had been signed. He drove us then to the cemetery and we all remembered Elia intensely…

By evening, a nice surprise awaited me: The family threw a farewell party for me, under a sign "Gracias, Don Pablo, siempre lo recordaremos" [Thank you, Pablo, we will always remember you]—very moving: my frequent help was appreciated after all!

Sunday morning, after sad good-byes to family and neighbours, I took the bus with Paul to La Ceiba, to see his aunt Betina (through whom my support payments to him and his grandmother flow) and discuss his future. Having missed out on the Academy, he finally decided to study Civil Engineering at the local campus, where now he can take classes at home. After a fond farewell there, Paul escorted me all the way to El Progreso, where we had to part quickly so that he could still catch the last bus back to Olanchito.

I spent a final night at good old HPV (Hotel Plaza Victoria), where the owner couple Vasquez treats me like family, as I, and later Elia, have stayed there a good many times over the last 25 years. Their daughter is the widow of the lawyer who helped me to become a resident of Honduras, and she is now the executor of my will for Paul. Elia and I had our wedding reception there, and I left a plaque of recommendation on their counter. On Monday 3 February 2020 I went away with a heavy heart; faithful taxi driver Tomas took me to the airport, and I left Honduras for good…

I had developed quite a cough there the last few days, which ballooned into a nasty bronchitis that took over a month and anti-biotics to overcome. One can only marvel at God's exquisite timing: Four weeks later, Covid-19 arrived in Canada and elsewhere, and I could easily have been marooned in Honduras and/or been infected myself.

Thus ended my long involvement with Latin America that had begun with my Beetle-trip through the length of the continent in 1958, continued with ten visits (including one by bicycle) to my various foster children in Central America between 1979 and 2000, intensified with well over a hundred medical missions to Central and South America during the years from 1984 to 2020, and culminated in almost twenty years of married life in Honduras that ended with Elia's untimely death in 2019. Now the only direct link that remains is with son Paul and memories…

As the current patriarch of the family, its extension is of great interest to me. It is a strange genealogical fact that in the Loofs-family—which we can trace back to the 17th Century, to Adam Loofs (a Dutch silver/goldsmith who served Willem of Orange)—no matter how many sons were born in the following generations, only one would carry on the family name. That is true right up to now: Of us three brothers, only Helmut had a son (who has two now). The original Dutch line has died out long ago, and the German branch ended with the emigration of both surviving brothers as a consequence of WWII. While the Canadian branch will come to an end with me, the prospects for continuation are good in Australia and also Honduras. Interesting cross-overs for future DNA-researches to unrevel…

Going back a bit to recent times, after my sister Friederun died in Germany in April 2016 (aged 95), then came our "anno horribilis" 2018/19, when within six months I lost my first wife Anneliese in Canada in July, my brother Helmut in Australia in August, and then my wife Elia in Honduras in the following January. Thus both my sisters, both my brothers, and both my wives have predeceased me. I am so glad that Anneliese and I had reconciled gloriously in the Summer of 2016 (after 40 years of not seeing each other), to the joy of ourselves and our daughters. Likewise, I am grateful that the Lord let me make that last trip to Germany in September of 2019, to see my birth place, attend the AGM of the venerable Thomas School in Leipzig (to which we three brothers all went), and spend a few days with my nieces' families in Detmold and Colditz.

Brother-in-law Armin is still alive there (at 95), but has lost both his sons to cancer, in 2012 and in 2020. Sister-in-law Sigi in Australia suffered a severe stroke at 82 and has died there in January 2021. My own daughter Brigit underwent risky surgery to remove a brain tumour, but is recovering nicely—one thing or another, as people get older. Though I am otherwise in relatively good health, my prostate cancer is acting up again, but after many good years and me now pushing 93, I cannot complain. What is hard is the interruption of family visits due to the pandemic and travel restrictions. Like so many others, I had to cancel my traditional pre-Christmas visits to Ottawa—the first time in 30 years that I could not see my daughters, nor the son in Honduras for that matter. What anguish for many parents, and what fear for old folks, to perhaps to have to suffer and die alone…

But as Christians we live on hope and faith in the Lord's guidance. Also, like St. Paul said to the Philippians (4, 11), I have learned to be content in whatever circumstances. I rely on Proverbs 3, 5 "Trust in the Lord with all your heart", rather than trying to answer the "why?" question—God has all the answers, we must wait.

All the above events in my life will have shown the reader how many times merciful intervention by God or His angels have saved me in dicey situations. Without divine providence, I could not have extricated myself from these situations, or may not even have survived. Now that I am approaching the end, I want to close with Verse 4 of the famous Psalm 23: 4.

Even though I walk through the darkest valley,
I fear no evil;
for you are with me;
your rod and your staff—
they comfort me.

Praise and thanks be to God!

The last Honduran family photo, Olanchito, taken on Paul's 19th birthday, six weeks before Elia's untimely death, Nov 2018

The latest Canadian family photo, Ottawa, Sept 2021
L-R: Brigit, the author (at 92), Karen

Epilogue

Now that I'm in my early nineties, when I look back over my life, a feeling of profound gratitude comes over me that God has protected and guided me all that time. He let me survive the Second World War and the post-war chaos, steering me to a good life in Canada. He also let me see much of His creation, holding His hands over me on my often risky and long travels. Moreover, He has kept me largely in good health, a huge favour and totally undeserved. How many of my generation perished innocently on land, at sea, in the air, or were maimed or left destitute for life! How much poverty, sickness, and misery have I seen myself in the third world, notably on my many medical missions to Latin America, but also privately in my third home country of Honduras!

As before in wartime, the question "Why they and not us?" forces itself on my mind. In particular, how can one justify our lifestyle, shaped by consumerism and materialism, in the face of over half the population of the world living in poverty? This situation has weighed on my mind for years and driven home the point that we in the developed world in general, and Christians in particular, have a moral obligation to help the worse-off and live our own lives at a defensible and sustainable level. Though even Jesus said that the poor will always be with us, I believe that each one of us can do something to alleviate some of the misery. I have tried to do just that.

In my more than ninety years, I have seen many changes, especially in technology. Where have the Zeppelins, steam locomotives, and tube radios of my youth gone? On the other hand, we now have television, computers, smart phones and social media. Are they all good, or even necessary, and where does all that lead to? In the face of social changes and an increasingly secular world, it's hard to be optimistic—unless we get back to the Bible, and practice its Christian love and values.

In the book of Hebrews (13:5) we are told to be *"content with what you have"*, and I certainly am, although—or possibly because—I have always lived simply and within my means. Thanks to the Lord's help and that of His angels, my upbringing, education, and good health, I have been able to see much of the world, traversing all continents on land (except Antarctica) and all oceans by boat (except the Arctic). On my travels and in my charity work, I have met people of many cultures and gained good friends. In my two marriages with good women, I have shared joys and sorrows and helped bring up my two daughters and a son. I have tried to be a father figure for nine foster children, and generally to do my bit to make this a better world.

Indeed, this has been a rich life, but it is not quite over yet. Apparently the Lord still has work for me. Each year that He grants me I will use for the good of my family and my biblical neighbour in this world, until called into the next. Amen.

In His Hands

The author's travels in Europe in 1950 and 51 are shown in white dotted lines. The large dots indicate the 1951 bicycle trip through southern countries. Map published in Cominco Magazine, June 1954 issue, page 14. Used by permission.

The author's bicycle trip through Central America in 1982 to visit four SOS Children's villages (as underlined). Map drawn by the author.

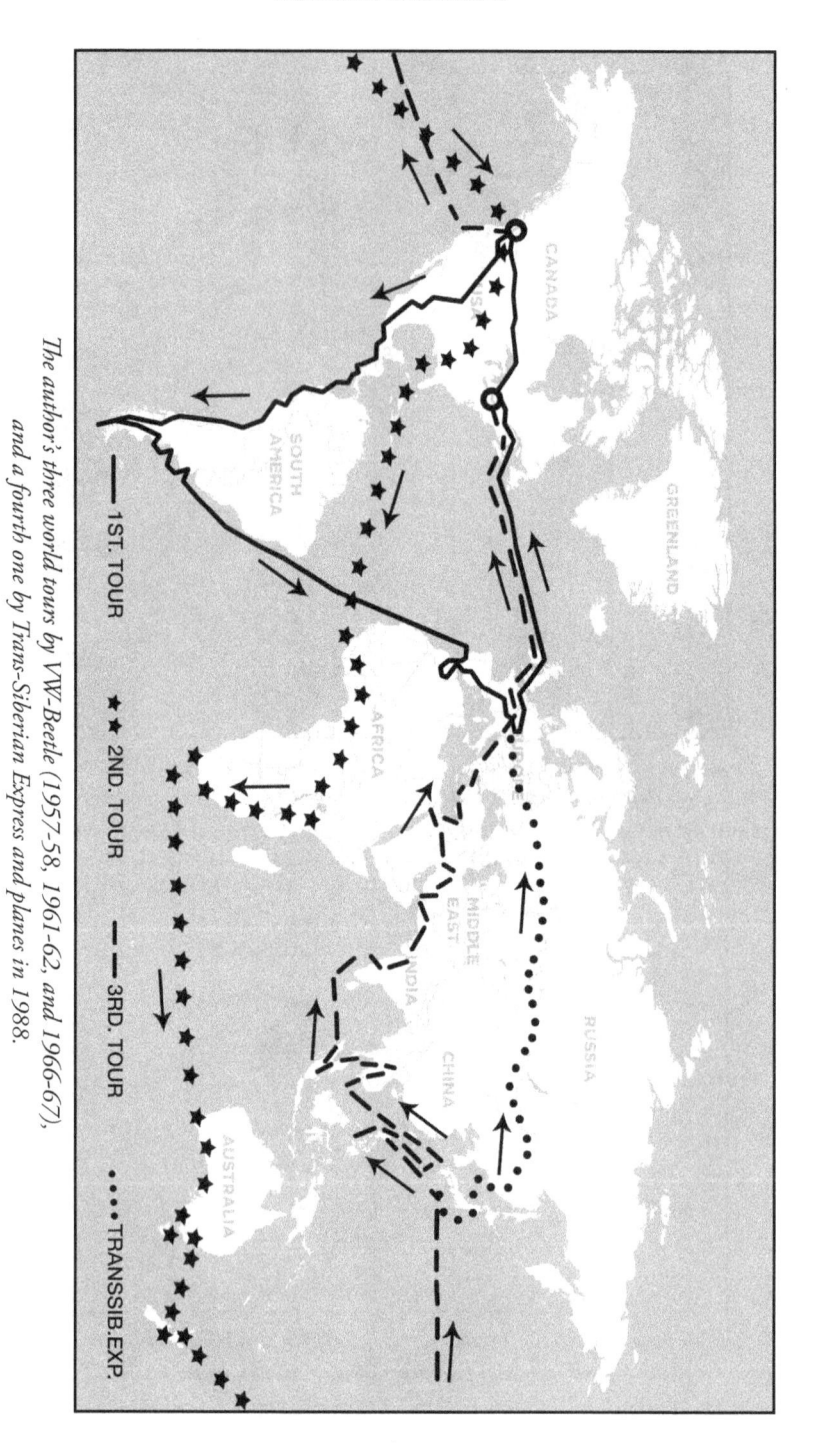

The author's three world tours by VW-Beetle (1957-58, 1961-62, and 1966-67), and a fourth one by Trans-Siberian Express and planes in 1988.

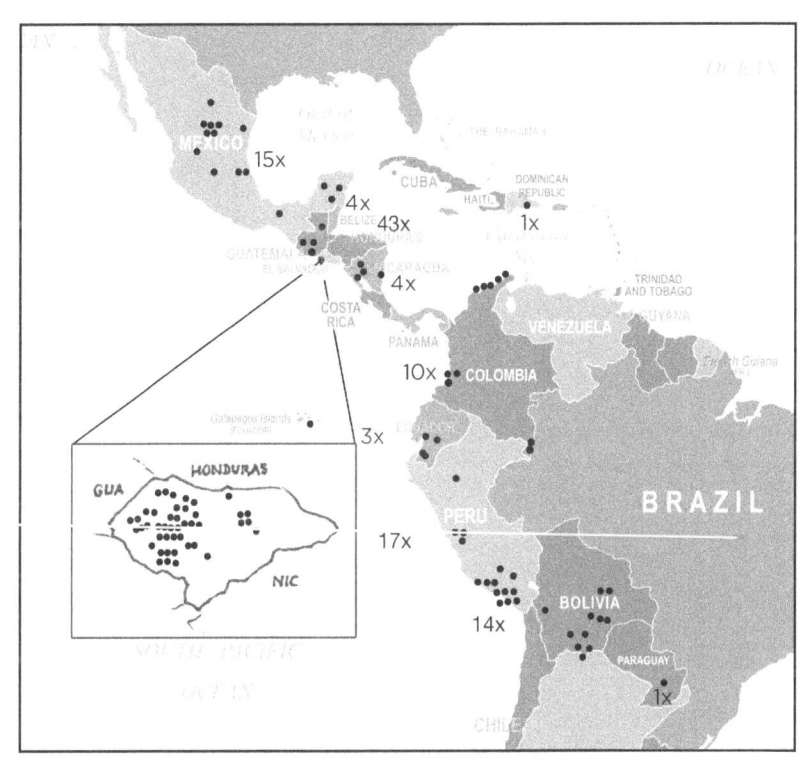

My 112 (54/58) Med/Eye Missions in Latin America, 1984-2020: Location (dots) and number (x) per country.

C Am=67		S Am=45	
Honduras	43	Peru	17
Mexico	15	Bolivia	14
Nicaragua	4	Colombia	10
Guatemala	4	Ecuador	3
Dom. Rep.	1	Paraguay	1

CPSIA information can be obtained
at www.ICGtesting.com
Printed in the USA
BVHW041914261122
652729BV00001B/17

9 781486 623648